I0017891

Geospatial Database Management System

Geo Report

2023

Preface

Navigating the Future with Geo Report

Dear reader,

It is with great pleasure that we welcome you to the world of technology, geospatial data analysis, and continuing education through this book. Here, you will come into contact with the most advanced concepts and the most up-to-date information in a constantly evolving scenario, guided by Geo Report, a company passionate about education and innovation.

Geo Report is much more than just a company; is a project whose mission is to illuminate the path of those who wish to explore the frontier of knowledge. Founded as an EdTech and GISTech, Geo Report offers services ranging from generating intelligence reports to producing educational resources that empower individuals and organizations to meet the challenges of the modern world.

Geospatial Data Intelligence and Analysis Reports: Imagine making strategic decisions based on accurate and up-to-date information. Geo Report uses cutting-edge technology to help companies and organizations transform geospatial data into valuable insights, providing significant competitive advantages.

Continuing Education: Learning is a never-ending journey, and Geo Report is committed to being your guide on this journey. Our books and educational materials promote both basic concepts and advanced knowledge about technology, supporting students, professionals and enthusiasts looking to improve and thrive in a world driven by innovation.

Technological Update: In the ever-changing world of technology, being out of date can be a critical disadvantage. Geo Report keeps a close eye on emerging technology trends and shares this information with you, ensuring you are always one step ahead.

This book is just one of the many tools Geo Report offers to enable you to navigate the vast ocean of technology. As you flip through these pages, you prepare to embark on a journey that will lead you to discover the power of geospatial data analysis, understand essential technology concepts, and stay up to date on the latest innovations.

As you dive into the content of this book, remember that Geo Report is at your side, ready to guide and support you in your quest for knowledge and technological excellence. The future is your blank canvas, and we're here to help you paint the brightest picture possible.

Happy studying and a learning journey full of discoveries!

Yours sincerely,

Geo Report Collaborators

Chapter 1: Introduction to Geospatial Database Management Systems

1.1. What is a Geospatial Database?

A Geospatial Database, in simple terms, is an information storage system that deals with data related to geographic locations. Its fundamental function is to organize and store information that has some connection to specific places on Earth.

Imagine you have a digital map on your phone. This map uses a Geospatial Database to store information about roads, buildings, points of interest and more. When you search for a nearby restaurant or get directions to a destination, the Geospatial Database helps you find and display that information in the correct location on the map.

A Geospatial Database helps maintain and access information related to geographic locations, making it easier for us to understand, navigate, and make decisions based on location. It is essential in many applications such as GPS systems, urban planning, precision agriculture and more.

1.2. Importance of Geospatial Management

Geospatial management plays a vital role today due to its growing importance in several areas. It involves the collection, storage, analysis and presentation of data related to geographic locations and is critical for several reasons, providing a range of benefits in areas such as urban planning, agriculture and decision-making. Here are some reasons why geospatial management is so important:

1. Efficient Urban Planning: In the context of growing cities, geospatial management assists in the analysis of data on land use, infrastructure and transport. This allows for more efficient urban planning, resulting in more sustainable, accessible and pleasant cities for residents.

2. Precision Agriculture: Modern agriculture relies heavily on geospatial management. Farmers use geospatial data to optimize irrigation, fertilizer and pesticide application, and monitor crops. This increases productivity and reduces wasted resources.

3. Natural Resource Management: The conservation of natural resources, such as forests, rivers and protected areas, depends on geospatial management. Geospatial

data helps identify critical areas for biodiversity and sustainably manage these resources.

4. Public Safety and Disaster Response: In emergency situations, such as natural disasters or public health crises, geospatial management allows for a quick and effective response. Locating affected areas, coordinating rescue efforts and distributing resources becomes much more efficient.

5. Data-Driven Decision Making: For governments and businesses, making informed decisions is essential. Geospatial management provides accurate data on markets, resource distribution and competition analysis, making decisions more solid.

6. Transportation and Logistics: Transport and logistics companies use geospatial data to optimize routes, reduce costs and improve the delivery of goods. This benefits both companies and consumers.

7. Asset Management: Companies that have geographically distributed assets, such as energy networks, gas pipelines and telecommunications, rely on geospatial management to track, maintain and update these assets effectively.

8. Environment and Conservation: The study of climate change, biodiversity conservation and environmental impact analysis depend on geospatial data. They help identify trends and target conservation efforts.

Geospatial management unlocks a wealth of valuable information about our world, enabling us to make smarter, more sustainable decisions across a wide range of areas. As technology advances, the importance of geospatial management will continue to grow, offering increasingly innovative and impactful solutions to the challenges of our time.

1.3. Geospatial Database Management Systems Applications

Geospatial database management systems (Geospatial DBMS) have a wide range of applications across various industries, taking advantage of the ability to store, analyze and visualize information based on geographic location. Here are some of the practical applications in different industries:

1. Geography and Cartography:
   - Topographic Mapping: Geospatial DBMSs are used to create accurate topographic maps, showing terrain details, elevations and geographic features.
   - Map Update: Allows continuous updating of maps with real-time information, such as changes in public roads and buildings.

2. Navigation and GPS:

- Vehicle Navigation: GPS systems use Geospatial DBMS to provide accurate driving guidance and real-time traffic information.
- Outdoor Navigation: Assist with activities such as hiking, climbing and cycling, offering interactive maps and precise coordinates.

3. Environment:
- Environmental Monitoring: Used to track air and water pollution, deforestation, climate change and species migration patterns.
- Natural Resource Management: They help manage resources such as forests, natural parks and reserves, facilitating conservation.

4. Agriculture:
- Precision Agriculture: Allows crop monitoring, soil analysis and precise application of agricultural resources, increasing productivity and reducing costs.
- Agricultural Zoning: They help identify suitable areas for growing specific crops.

5. Marketing and Commerce:
- Market Analysis: Facilitates analysis of the location of customers, competitors and points of sale, helping companies make expansion and marketing decisions.
- Geomarketing: Personalize marketing campaigns based on customers' location, offering targeted promotions and offers.

6. Urban and Real Estate Planning:

- Urban Zoning: Used to plan land use, residential and commercial zones, and identify development areas.
- Real Estate Appraisal: They help determine the value of properties based on geographic factors, such as location and accessibility.

7. Transportation and Logistics:
- Routing and Logistics: Optimize transport routes, reduce fuel costs and improve delivery efficiency.
- Asset Tracking: Allows real-time tracking of vehicles, cargo and assets in transit.

8. Public Health:
- Epidemiology: They help map the spread of diseases, identify high-risk areas and plan vaccination campaigns.
- Health Resource Management: Assist in the allocation of medical resources based on population density and geographic needs.

These are just some of the many applications of Geospatial DBMSs. As geospatial technology and data continue to evolve, new opportunities and solutions are constantly emerging across industries, improving efficiency, decision-making, and understanding of the world around us.

1.4. Challenges in Geospatial Data Management

Geospatial data management, although a fundamental part of modern technology, faces several challenges that can complicate the collection, storage and effective use of this information. Here are some of the common challenges and ways to overcome them:

1. Data Accuracy:
  - Challenge: The accuracy of geospatial data is critical, especially in applications such as navigation, precision agriculture and environmental analysis. Location errors can have significant consequences.
  - Overcoming the Challenge: Accurate data collection is critical. This can be achieved through advanced sensing technologies, such as high-precision GPS, and constant validation of data with reliable sources. Furthermore, error correction must be incorporated into processes.

2. System Interoperability:
  - Challenge: Different systems and platforms often use different geospatial data formats, making integration and information exchange between them difficult.
  - Overcoming the Challenge: Standardization is crucial. Using open standards, such as the Shapefile format or the GeoJSON standard, helps ensure that data can be shared and integrated more effectively. Furthermore, the implementation of interoperability

protocols, such as OGC (Open Geospatial Consortium), facilitates communication between systems.

3. Privacy and Security Issues:
   - Challenge: Geospatial data often includes sensitive information, such as the location of homes and businesses. Ensuring the privacy and security of this data is crucial.
   - Overcoming the Challenge: Anonymizing data is a common approach to protecting privacy. This involves removing or obfuscating personally identifiable information. Additionally, implementing cybersecurity measures such as encryption and authentication helps protect sensitive data from unauthorized access.

4. Data Volume and Speed:
   - Challenge: With the proliferation of mobile devices, sensors and data collection technologies, the amount of geospatial information generated is immense. Dealing with large volumes of data in real time can be challenging.
   - Overcoming the Challenge: Cloud computing and distributed processing are viable solutions for dealing with large volumes of data. Additionally, compression algorithms and streaming data management techniques can help deal with the speed of real-time data.

5. Costs and Data Access:
   - Challenge: Acquiring and maintaining high-quality geospatial data can be expensive. Additionally, access to quality data may be limited in some regions.

- Overcoming the Challenge: Public-private partnerships can help share costs and resources for data collection. Furthermore, open data policies can make basic geospatial information more accessible, benefiting a wide range of users.

Overcoming these challenges in geospatial data management requires a collaborative effort from governments, companies and research communities. Constant technological innovation and awareness of quality, interoperability and security issues are crucial to fully leveraging the power of geospatial data in our everyday lives and critical applications.

1.5. Chapter Overview

This book offers a comprehensive and in-depth exploration of the world of geospatial database management systems. Over the next few chapters, we will delve into a journey that ranges from the fundamentals of geospatial data to its practical application in various sectors. Initially, we focus on establishing a solid understanding of the nature of geospatial data and how it is modeled. We then explore essential tools and techniques for spatial queries, data import/export, and integration with other applications. We also address challenges and critical considerations, such as safety, ethics and future trends. With illustrative case studies and practical examples, this book is designed to help readers master the use of Geospatial Database Management Systems and understand their transformative impact on a variety of industries, from urban planning and agriculture to marketing and environmental preservation. Get ready for an exciting journey through the vast world of geospatial data and its interdisciplinary applications.

Chapter 2: Geospatial Data Fundamentals

2.1. Geospatial Data and its Nature

Geospatial data, also known as spatial data or geodata, refers to information that is directly associated with a specific geographic location on Earth. This data is characterized by its unique nature, which is based on geographic coordinates, such as latitude and longitude, to describe the position of objects, events or phenomena on the Earth's surface. Here are some distinguishing characteristics of geospatial data:

1. Geographic Location: The fundamental characteristic of geospatial data is its direct association with a specific geographic location. Each point or element in the data has geographic coordinates that uniquely identify it in relation to the Earth's surface.

2. Variety of Data Types: Geospatial data can represent a wide variety of information, including points of interest, roads, borders, terrain elevations, vegetation cover, weather data, and more. This diversity of data types allows detailed information about the natural and built environment to be captured and analyzed.

3. Dynamic Character: Geospatial data can be static, such as the location of a city, or dynamic, such as the constantly changing position of a moving vehicle. This

allows for real-time tracking and analysis of movements and trends.

4. Spatial Reference: Geospatial data is spatially referenced using geographic coordinate systems, cartographic projection systems and other methods that allow the accurate representation of the Earth's surface on maps and geographic information systems (GIS).

5. Diverse Applications: Due to its ability to represent information in a location context, geospatial data is essential in a wide variety of applications such as urban planning, precision agriculture, GPS navigation, environmental monitoring, logistics, marketing, epidemiological analysis and much more. They provide valuable insights for decision-making and problem-solving in many fields.

6. Data Integration: Geospatial data is often integrated with other data sources, such as demographic, economic or social data. This integration enriches the understanding of the contexts in which geospatial events or objects occur.

Geospatial data is information that has geographic coordinates and is intrinsically linked to its location on Earth. This data plays a fundamental role in a wide range of applications, enabling the analysis of geographic patterns, decision-making support and the ability to better understand the world around us, making it a valuable tool in our daily lives and across many disciplines. .

2.2. Geographic Coordinate Systems

Geographic coordinate systems are reference systems that allow the precise and unique representation of points or locations on the Earth's surface. These systems are essential for cartography, navigation, geodesy, geospatial analysis and many other applications that depend on the accurate description of geographic position. They work by combining two main coordinates: latitude and longitude.

- Latitude: Latitude is the coordinate that measures the distance of a point in relation to the Equator. It varies from -90° (at the South Pole) to +90° (at the North Pole). Points on the Equator have a latitude of 0°, and latitude increases as we move toward the poles.

- Longitude: Longitude is the coordinate that measures the distance of a point in relation to the Greenwich Meridian, which is considered the reference point for longitude. It ranges from -180° (west of the Greenwich Meridian) to +180° (east of the Greenwich Meridian). Points on the Greenwich Meridian itself have a longitude of 0°, and longitude increases both east and west of the meridian.

By combining latitude and longitude, we can accurately determine the location of any point on the Earth's surface. For example, New York City has a latitude of approximately 40.7128°N (40.7128 degrees north of the Equator) and a longitude of approximately 74.0060°W (74.0060 degrees west of Greenwich).

In addition to geographic coordinates, there are other geodetic coordinate systems, such as the UTM (Universal Transverse Mercator) system, which divides the Earth into zones and uses Cartesian coordinates to represent locations within each zone. Other systems, such as geocentric coordinates, are used in advanced geodesy and scientific applications.

Geographic coordinate systems are the basis for representing points on the Earth's surface. They provide an accurate and universally recognized way of describing geographic locations, facilitating navigation, cartography, and a variety of applications that rely on location information.

2.3. Geospatial Data Representation

Geospatial data representation plays a fundamental role in understanding and communicating information about the Earth. There are several ways to represent this data, each with its own advantages and disadvantages. Here are some of the main forms of representation:

1. Maps:
    - Advantages: Maps provide a direct visual representation of Earth's geography, allowing people to see the spatial distribution of resources, political boundaries, natural features, and more. They are widely used in navigation, urban planning and geographic education.
    - Disadvantages: The scale of maps can affect the accuracy of the representation, and certain geographic features can be simplified or distorted. Additionally, updating maps can be a time-consuming process.

2. Satellite Images:
    - Advantages: Satellite images offer a detailed and updated view of the Earth's surface. They are useful in environmental monitoring, weather forecasting, precision agriculture and urban analysis.
    - Disadvantages: Availability and resolution of images may vary. Additionally, weather conditions and cloud cover can affect image quality.

3. Digital Terrain Models (DTM):
    - Advantages: MDTs represent the Earth's topography with precise details. They are used in infrastructure planning, visibility analysis, flood simulation and more.
    - Disadvantages: Creating MDTs requires topographic surveys or data from remote sensors, which can be

expensive and time-consuming. Furthermore, the resolution of MDTs may vary.

4. Geographical Information Systems (GIS):
   - Advantages: GIS allow the integration and analysis of different types of geospatial data on a single platform. They are highly flexible and customizable and are used in a wide range of applications, from urban planning to market analysis.
   - Disadvantages: GIS implementation and maintenance can be complex and require specialized training. Furthermore, the quality of the results depends on the quality of the input data.

5. Virtual Reality and Augmented Reality:
   - Advantages: These technologies allow for an immersive experience that combines geospatial data with the real world. They are used in education, tourism, military training and project visualization.
   - Disadvantages: Require specialized hardware, such as virtual reality glasses or smartphones with augmented reality capabilities. Additionally, the accuracy of real-world data overlay may vary.

   Each method of representing geospatial data has its appropriate place and application, and the choice depends on specific project needs and resource limitations. Often, a combination of various forms of representation is used to gain a comprehensive understanding of the geographic environment and support informed decisions across a variety of industries.

2.4. Geospatial Data Types

Geospatial data can be divided into two main types: vector data and matrix data. Each type has its distinct characteristics and applications in different real-world contexts:

1. Vector Data:
   - Characteristics: Vector data represents geospatial information through discrete geometric objects, such as points, lines and polygons. Each object is defined by geographic coordinates (latitude and longitude) and associated attributes, such as name, population, category, etc.
   - Application Examples:
   - Road Maps: Vector data is used to represent road networks, with detailed information about roads, intersections and landmarks.
   - Municipal Registries: They are used to map properties, their borders and information about the property, such as owner and assessed value.

- Urban Planning: Allows the representation of land use zones, green areas, administrative limits and urban infrastructure.
- Telecommunications Networks: They are used to map the location of cell towers, fiber optic cables and internet access points.

2. Matrix Data:
- Characteristics: Matrix data represents geospatial information as a grid of cells, where each cell has an associated value or attribute. These grids can represent various information, such as terrain elevation, temperature, precipitation and satellite images.
- Application Examples:
- Digital Elevation Modeling (DEM): DEM matrix data represents the Earth's topography, being used in flood simulations, road planning and visibility analysis.
- Satellite Images: Matrix data from satellite images are widely used in environmental monitoring, detection of changes in land cover, precision agriculture and weather forecasting.
- Land Use Maps: They represent land cover in a grid of cells, being useful in analyzes of land use change and urban planning.
- Climate Data: Matrix data can represent climate variables such as temperature, humidity and precipitation, being crucial for climate predictions and environmental impact studies.

The choice between vector and matrix data depends on the nature of the data, the needs of the application and the accuracy required. While vector data is ideal for representing well-defined features such as roads and borders, raster data is better suited for representing continuous phenomena such as terrain elevation and weather data. In many cases, a combination of both types of data is used to obtain a comprehensive view of the geospatial environment.

2.5. Geospatial Data Quality

The quality of geospatial data plays a key role in all applications that rely on location information, from navigation and urban planning to environmental monitoring and market analysis. Data quality refers to the accuracy, completeness, timeliness and reliability of geospatial information. Here are the main factors that can affect the quality of geospatial data:

1. Accuracy:
    - Accuracy refers to the proximity between the geospatial location recorded in the data and the actual location on the ground. Inaccurate data can lead to significant errors in applications such as navigation, precision agriculture and environmental monitoring.

2. Integrity:
    - Data integrity involves the consistency and completeness of geospatial information. Incomplete or

inconsistent data can lead to misinterpretations and inappropriate decisions.

3. Update:
- Freshness refers to how frequently data is updated to reflect changes in the real world. Out-of-date data can be problematic in situations where conditions change rapidly, such as natural disasters or urban development.

4. Data Source:
- The quality of geospatial data often depends on the source from which it was collected. High-quality data generally comes from reliable sources, such as accurate topographic surveys or high-resolution satellite imagery.

5. Scanning and Processing Errors:
- Errors introduced during scanning, storing and processing data can affect its quality. It is important to minimize these errors through validation and quality control techniques.

6. Resolution and Scale:
- The resolution of geospatial data also influences its quality. Low-resolution data may not capture important details, while high-resolution data may be excessively detailed for some applications.

The quality of geospatial data is critical in location-based decisions, as errors or inaccurate information can have serious consequences. For example, in a navigation system, a lack of accuracy can lead a vehicle onto the wrong road, while in precision agriculture, inaccuracy in planting data can result in excessive use of resources such as water and fertilizers.

Furthermore, in urban analytics, data quality affects infrastructure planning and land use zoning. In environmental monitoring, low-quality data can lead to inappropriate decisions that affect the conservation and management of natural resources.

Therefore, ensuring the quality of geospatial data is essential to obtain accurate and reliable results in a variety of applications that depend on location information, benefiting decision-making and efficiency in several areas.

Chapter 3: Geospatial Data Modeling

3.1. Conceptual Modeling of Geospatial Data

Conceptual modeling of geospatial data is a fundamental step in the process of developing geographic information systems (GIS) and managing geospatial data. This step focuses on creating an abstract, conceptual representation of the data and its relationships, without worrying about technical implementation details such as the underlying database structure.

Here are the key aspects of conceptual geospatial data modeling:

1. Data Abstraction: In conceptual modeling, geospatial data are represented in an abstract way, that is, they are described in terms of their concepts and characteristics without worrying about how this data will be stored or accessed in a real system .

2. Entities and Relationships: During this stage, the main entities (objects or concepts) that make up the geospatial domain in question are identified. Furthermore, the relationships between these entities are defined, highlighting how they relate and interact with each other.

3. Attributes: The attributes associated with entities are also identified and defined. This includes specific information that describes each entity. For example, in a conceptual model for a public transport system, entities might include "subway stations" and "bus routes", with attributes such as "station name" and "bus departure times".

4. Hierarchies and Aggregations: Conceptual models can also include hierarchies and aggregations to organize data logically. For example, a model might represent "countries" as aggregations of "states", and "states" as aggregations of "counties".

5. Diagrams and Notations: The representation of conceptual modeling often involves the use of diagrams and graphic notations. Entity-relationship diagrams (DER) and UML (Unified Modeling Language) diagrams are commonly used to visualize entities, relationships and attributes in a clear and understandable way.

Conceptual modeling of geospatial data is crucial to ensuring that the requirements and concepts underlying the geographic domain are accurately understood and documented. This initial abstraction helps define the logical structure of the data before beginning technical implementation in a geographic information system (GIS) or geospatial database. This helps to avoid problems and rework later in system development, allowing a solid foundation for creating effective and accurate geospatial applications.

3.2. Logical Modeling of Geospatial Data

Logical modeling of geospatial data is the second crucial step in developing geographic information systems (GIS) and managing geospatial data. After creating conceptual modeling, which abstractly represents data and its relationships, logical modeling focuses on translating this conceptual representation into a logical, structured format that can be implemented in a database system. Here is a more detailed explanation of the geospatial data logical modeling process:

1. Identification of Entities and Attributes: In logical modeling, the entities and attributes identified in the conceptual phase are refined and detailed. This involves precisely defining the tables or classes that will represent the entities and their corresponding attributes. For example, if the conceptual entity was "subway stations" with attributes such as "name" and "location", in logical modeling you would define a "Subway Stations" table with columns for each attribute.

2. Definition of Relationships: Relationships between entities are also translated into logical relationships in databases. For example, if there was a "connects to" relationship between "subway stations" and "bus routes", that relationship would be implemented through

foreign keys or other relationship mechanisms in a relational database.

3. Choice of Data Types: Logical modeling requires choosing the appropriate data types for each attribute. This includes deciding whether an attribute will be a text string, a number, a date, a spatial object (such as a point or polygon), among others. The choice of data types affects storage efficiency and query performance.

4. Definition of Indexes: To optimize the performance of queries on geospatial data, it is common to create indexes on relevant fields. For example, if you want to quickly query all subway stations in a specific city, you can create an index on the geographic location column.

5. Selection of Database Management System (DBMS): The choice of DBMS is crucial in logical modeling. Geospatial DBMSs, such as PostgreSQL with spatial extensions (PostGIS) or Oracle Spatial, are often used to store geospatial data due to their ability to handle complex spatial data types.

6. Data Normalization: Normalization is a process that helps eliminate redundancies and maintain data integrity. It involves organizing tables to minimize duplication of information.

7. Validation and Review: Before proceeding with implementation, logical modeling goes through a validation and review phase to ensure that all

relationships, foreign keys and integrity constraints are correctly defined.

Logical modeling of geospatial data is a critical step that sets the stage for practical implementation of the data in a database system. It ensures that the database structure is designed to meet the requirements for storing and querying geospatial data efficiently and accurately, ensuring the integrity and reliability of geographic data throughout the application.

3.3. Physical Modeling of Geospatial Data

Physical modeling of geospatial data is the final step in the process of developing geographic information systems (GIS) and managing geospatial data. At this stage, attention turns to defining how data will be physically stored in a database system, considering crucial aspects of performance, efficiency and optimization. Here are the key elements of physical modeling of geospatial data:

1. Selection of Storage Structures: In the physical modeling stage, the storage structures that best suit the types of geospatial data to be stored are selected. This includes choosing tables, indexes, and other storage objects.

2. Choosing Spatial Data Types: A critical aspect of physically modeling geospatial data is the selection of appropriate spatial data types to represent geographic geometries. The types of spatial data vary depending on the database management system (DBMS) chosen, such as points, lines, polygons or even more complex objects.

3. Spatial Indexes: To speed up spatial queries, specific spatial indexes are created. These indexes help optimize geospatial data retrieval, allowing the DBMS to perform queries more efficiently. Common spatial indices include R-tree and quadtree indices.

4. Table Partitioning: In systems with large volumes of geospatial data, it may be necessary to divide tables into partitions to facilitate management and improve performance. This is especially useful for data that is frequently accessed by geographic region.

5. Query Optimization: During physical modeling, spatial query optimization techniques are considered. This involves analyzing the execution plan of queries to ensure they are efficient in terms of data access.

6. Metadata Storage: In addition to spatial data, metadata information, such as information about coordinate projections and update dates, is also physically stored.

7. Performance Considerations: Performance aspects are taken into consideration, such as choosing the storage location for geospatial data on disk, configuring caches and optimizing frequent queries.

8. Security and Access Control: Physical modeling also considers security aspects, such as defining access permissions to geospatial data to ensure that only authorized users can access it.

Physical modeling of geospatial data is critical to ensuring that geographic information systems (GIS) and geospatial databases function efficiently and meet specific spatial data storage and retrieval needs. Careful optimization at this stage can have a significant impact on query performance and system responsiveness, ensuring that geospatial data is managed effectively and efficiently.

3.4. Spatial Databases

Spatial databases are database management systems (DBMSs) specifically designed to store, manage and query geospatial data, that is, data that is directly associated with geographic locations on Earth. They differ from traditional databases in several important ways because of their ability to handle complex spatial information. Here are the main distinctions and functionalities of spatial databases:

1. Spatial Data Type Support: Spatial databases support native spatial data types such as points, lines, polygons, and more complex geometries, enabling accurate representation of geographic objects and phenomena.

2. Spatial Indexes: They include optimized spatial indexes, such as R-tree or quadtree indexes, that speed up spatial queries, allowing fast data retrieval based on location criteria.

3. Spatial Functions: Spatial databases provide a set of spatial functions that allow you to perform geospatial operations, such as calculations of distance, areas, intersections and unions between geometries, facilitating complex analyses.

4. Cartographic Projections: They support the definition and transformation of cartographic projections so that geospatial data can be represented in different geographic coordinate systems.

5. Data Integration: Spatial databases allow the integration of geospatial data with non-spatial data, such as attribute tables, for more comprehensive analysis.

6. Georeferencing: They are capable of georeferencing data, associating non-geospatial information with geographic coordinates for consultation and subsequent analysis.

7. Spatial Queries: Support complex spatial queries, such as searching for nearby points of interest, identifying areas of overlap between polygons, and route calculations.

8. Geoprocessing: Many spatial databases include geoprocessing functionalities that enable advanced analysis, such as isoline analysis, terrain modeling, and geospatial simulations.

9. Spatial Metadata Management: They provide capabilities for storing and retrieving geospatial metadata, including information about data quality, source and projection.

10. Map Overview: Some spatial databases offer the ability to create map views directly from stored data, making it easier to graphically represent query results.

Spatial databases are designed to deal with the complexities of geospatial data, providing specific functionalities for storing, querying and analyzing this information. They play a key role in a variety of applications, from navigation systems to urban planning and environmental monitoring, enabling organizations to explore and utilize geospatial data effectively and accurately.

3.5. Spatial Indexing

Spatial indexing is a fundamental technique used in spatial database management systems (DBMSs) to accelerate the retrieval of geospatial data. It is based on the creation of special index structures that organize geospatial data in a way that facilitates efficient location queries and spatial analysis. The goal of spatial indexing is to reduce the time required to retrieve information based on location criteria, thereby improving the performance of spatial queries. Here are the main concepts and techniques related to spatial indexing:

1. Space Trees:
   - Spatial trees, such as the R-tree (R for "rectangle"), are one of the most common spatial indexing techniques. They organize data into a hierarchical tree structure, where tree nodes represent geographic regions that group spatial objects. This allows for quick location of objects within areas of interest, reducing the amount of data to be considered in each query.

2. Grid Indexes:
   - Grid indices divide geographic space into regular grid cells. Each geospatial object is associated with one or more grid cells. This method is simple and effective for proximity and intersection queries, but can lead to very large indexes in areas with high object density.

3. Quadtree:

- A quadtree is a hierarchical index structure that repeatedly divides space into four quadrants. It is effective for queries in specific regions of space and offers advantages over grid indexes in terms of adapting to varying densities of objects.

4. Hash Function Indices:
- Hash function indices apply hash functions to geospatial coordinates to organize data. While they are effective for equality queries, they are not as well suited for proximity or range queries.

5. Octrees:
- Octrees are similar to quadtrees, but divide three-dimensional space into eight octants instead of quadrants. They are used for spatial indexing in 3D environments, such as terrain visualization or three-dimensional analysis.

6. Scatter Page Indices:
- Scatter page indexes associate each object with a page on disk using hash functions. This helps in organizing geospatial objects on disks and improves access to geospatial data on disk storage systems.

The choice of spatial indexing technique depends on the specific application needs, data volume, and complexity of spatial queries. Many spatial DBMSs, such as PostGIS for PostgreSQL and Oracle Spatial, support several of these techniques, allowing developers to choose the one best suited to their needs. Spatial indexing is essential for ensuring efficient performance of spatial queries against geospatial databases, which is critical for a wide range of applications that rely on location information.

Chapter 4: Spatial Queries in Geospatial Databases

4.1. Basic Queries

Basic queries in geospatial databases refer to operations that allow you to retrieve fundamental information about data that has a geographic component. These consultations are essential for analysis and decision-making in various areas, from urban planning to environmental monitoring. Below are some key concepts and practical examples of basic queries in geospatial databases:

1. Proximity Consultation:
   - Concept: Retrieve geospatial objects that are close to a specific location.
   - Practical Example: Find restaurants that are within 1 km of a given geographic coordinate.

2. Intersection Query:
   - Concept: Retrieve geospatial objects that intersect with a given geographic region.
   - Practical Example: Identify all properties that intersect with the limits of a new urban development zone.

3. Containment Consultation:
   - Concept: Retrieve geospatial objects that are completely contained within a given geographic region.
   - Practical Example: Find all parks that are contained within the limits of a municipality.

4. Union Consultation:
   - Concept: Combine information from different geospatial data sets.
   - Practical Example: Merge population density data with land use data for urban planning analyses.

5. Attribute Selection Consultation:
   - Concept: Retrieve geospatial objects based on non-spatial attributes.
   - Practical Example: Select all public schools in a city with more than 500 students.

6. Buffer Query:
   - Concept: Create a zone of influence around a geospatial object (buffer) and recover objects that intersect this zone.
   - Practical Example: Identify all companies that are within a 2 km buffer around a new highway.

7. Space Grouping Consultation:
   - Concept: Group geospatial objects based on their spatial proximity.
   - Practical Example: Grouping parcel delivery points to optimize delivery routes.

8. Distance Measurement Consultation:
   - Concept: Measure the distance between two or more geospatial objects.
   - Practical Example: Calculate the distance between a store and its customers to optimize product distribution.

9. Spatial Overlay Query:

- Concept: Combine information from different spatial layers for more complex analyses.

- Practical Example: Use an overlay to identify areas that are simultaneously flood zones and places prone to landslides.

These basic queries form the basis for more advanced analysis in geospatial databases. The ability to perform these operations efficiently and accurately is crucial for extracting valuable insights and making informed decisions across diverse industries and applications.

4.2. Proximity Queries

Proximity queries in geospatial databases are essential tools for identifying elements that are close to a given geographic location. These queries enable the analysis of spatial relationships and are fundamental in various applications, from navigation to urban planning. Let's explore how these queries work and provide practical example usage scenarios.

Operation of Proximity Queries:

Proximity queries generally involve determining geospatial objects that are a certain distance (or within a radius) of a specific coordinate. To perform these queries, spatial database management systems (SGBD) use spatial indexes, such as R-trees, which organize data in a way that facilitates the efficient search for nearby elements.

Examples of Proximity Queries:

1. Find Nearby Establishments:
   - *Scenario:* An online mapping application allows users to find restaurants near a specific location.
   - *Query:* Retrieve all restaurants that are within 1 km of the coordinate of interest.

2. Mobile Asset Tracking:
   - *Scenario:* In logistics, track the proximity of delivery vehicles to a destination point.
   - *Consultation:* Identify all vehicles that are within 500 meters of a delivery point.

3. Environmental Monitoring:
   - *Scenario:* In an environmental monitoring system, identify data collection stations close to an area of interest.
   - *Query:* Retrieve all weather stations within a 2 km radius of a geographic coordinate.

4. Public Safety:
   - *Scenario:* In public safety applications, identify police stations close to an event or incident.

- *Consultation:* Retrieve all police stations that are within 3 km of an incident location.

5. Location of Points of Interest:
   - *Scenario:* A tourism application helps users find nearby tourist spots.
   - *Consultation:* Find all tourist attractions that are within 1.5 km of a given coordinate.

Benefits and Applications:

- Efficient Navigation: In navigation systems, proximity queries help identify points of interest, such as gas stations or restaurants, along a route.

- Urban Planning: Facilitate the identification of essential services, such as schools and hospitals, in relation to residential areas.

- Logistics and Tracking: These are essential for the efficient tracking of mobile assets, such as delivery vehicles.

- Security and Environmental Monitoring: Allows you to quickly locate relevant resources or monitoring stations in critical situations.

Proximity queries are crucial in geospatial environments, providing an effective way to identify and analyze nearby elements relative to a specific location. These consultations play a vital role across a variety of industries, improving service efficiency and providing a deeper understanding of spatial relationships.

4.3. Spatial Analysis Queries

Spatial analysis queries against geospatial databases are powerful tools that enable the exploration and understanding of complex patterns and relationships between geographic data. These queries go beyond basic operations, such as identifying elements near or within a specific area, and enable more sophisticated analyzes involving multiple layers of spatial data. Spatial analysis is critical in many areas, including urban planning, the environment, public health, and more.

Main Aspects of Spatial Analysis Queries:

1. Space Overlay:
   - *Concept:* It involves combining information from different spatial layers to identify areas of overlap or intersection.
   - *Practical Applications:* Identification of areas that simultaneously have specific characteristics, such as flood zones and natural habitats.

2. Buffer Analysis:

- *Concept:* It consists of creating surrounding zones (buffers) around geospatial elements to evaluate influences or spatial relationships.
    - *Practical Applications:* Assessment of environmental impacts around buildings or identification of locations affected by an incident.

3. Cluster Analysis:
    - *Concept:* Groups similar geographic elements based on spatial criteria.
    - *Practical Applications:* Identification of disease clusters in public health or customer grouping for market analysis.

4. Hotspot Analysis:
    - *Concept:* Identification of areas where the incidence of a phenomenon is significantly higher or lower than would be randomly expected.
    - *Practical Applications:* Identification of crime hotspots in a city.

5. Route Analysis:
    - *Concept:* Evaluation and optimization of routes based on spatial criteria, such as distance or travel time.
    - *Practical Applications:* Optimization of delivery routes or analysis of accessibility to health services.

6. Density Analysis:
    - *Concept:* Measures the concentration or dispersion of events or geographic elements in a specific area.

- *Practical Applications:* Assessment of population density or species distribution in ecology.

7. Spatial Correlation Analysis:
    - *Concept:* Evaluates the statistical relationship between spatial variables.
    - *Practical Applications:* Identification of correlations between the location of commercial establishments and consumption patterns.

8. Accessibility Analysis:
    - *Concept:* Assessment of the ease of reaching different locations based on spatial criteria.
    - *Practical Applications:* Public transport planning or analysis of accessibility to essential services.

Benefits and Practical Applications:

- Informed Decision Making: Spatial analysis provides valuable insights to support informed decisions in sectors such as urbanism, health, safety and environment.

- Identification of Complex Patterns: Allows the identification of complex spatial patterns that may not be evident in traditional analyses.

- Planning and Optimization: Facilitates efficient resource planning and operations optimization based on spatial considerations.

- Forecasting and Prevention: Helps in predicting trends and preventing problems, such as identifying areas prone to natural disasters.

Spatial analysis queries are crucial for in-depth understanding of geospatial data, providing a robust basis for making strategic decisions in a variety of contexts. These analyzes offer a richer perspective on spatial relationships, allowing organizations and researchers to explore and understand the complexity of geographic phenomena.

4.4. Temporal Queries

Temporal queries in geospatial databases are designed to deal with information that varies over time, enabling the analysis and retrieval of geospatial data with temporal dimensions. This approach is fundamental in many domains, such as environmental monitoring, urban planning, and natural resource management, where temporal dynamics play a critical role. Let's explore the concept of temporal queries and provide relevant examples:

Concept of Temporal Queries in Geospatial Databases:

Temporal queries involve the ability to analyze geospatial data considering its evolution over time. This means that information about geographic location is associated with temporal records, allowing not only the analysis of where something is, but also when it occurs. Temporality can be applied to a variety of data, such as changes in land use, population movements or climate variations.

Practical Examples of Temporal Queries:

1. Monitoring Changes in Land Use:
    - *Scenario:* A geospatial database maintains information about land use in a given region.
    - *Temporal Query:* Retrieve all changes in land cover in a specific area in the last five years, identifying urbanization patterns or environmental changes.

2. Animal Migration Monitoring:
    - *Scenario:* GPS tracking data of migratory animals is stored in a geospatial database.
    - *Temporal Consultation:* Analyze migration patterns throughout the seasons, identifying preferred routes and changes in feeding areas over time.

3. Dynamic Urban Planning:
    - *Scenario:* Data on buildings and urban infrastructure are maintained in a geospatial database.
    - *Temporal Consultation:* Evaluate urban growth over the last 20 years, identifying areas of expansion and planning future infrastructure needs.

4. Natural Disaster Analysis:
   - *Scenario:* Data on the history of climate events, such as hurricanes and floods, are recorded in a geospatial database.
   - *Temporal Consultation:* Analyze climate patterns over decades to identify trends and patterns in the occurrence of natural disasters.

5. Water Resources Management:
   - *Scenario:* Data on water quality in water bodies is stored in a geospatial database.
   - *Temporal Consultation:* Assess water quality throughout the seasons, identifying seasonal variations and potential impacts of human activities.

Benefits of Temporary Consultations:

- Trend Detection: Allows you to identify patterns and trends over time, facilitating informed decision-making.

- Response to Dynamic Events: Enables efficient response to dynamic events, such as natural disasters, through the analysis of time history.

- Dynamic Planning: Helps with dynamic planning, such as urban expansion, taking into account the temporal evolution of different variables.

- Sustainable Resource Management: Facilitates the sustainable management of natural resources by considering temporal variations in the use and quality of these resources.

Temporal queries against geospatial databases are essential for a comprehensive and dynamic understanding of the environment around us. They provide a temporal view that is crucial for analyzing patterns, detecting changes and efficiently managing resources in different contexts.

4.5. Spatial Query Optimization

Spatial query optimization is a crucial aspect in efficiently managing large geospatial datasets. With the increase in the availability of geographic information and the complexity of spatial queries, ensuring the efficient performance of these operations becomes essential for applications in several areas, including urban planning, navigation, environment and market analysis. Operational efficiency not only improves response speed, but also contributes to a smoother user experience and faster insights. Let's explore some strategies and techniques commonly used in optimizing spatial queries:

1. Use of Spatial Indexes:
   - Spatial indexes, such as R-tree or quadtree, are fundamental for accelerating spatial queries. They

organize data hierarchically, allowing quick retrieval of information based on location criteria.

2. Pre-Processing and Geometric Simplification:
   - Before running complex spatial queries, it is common to perform preprocessing steps such as geometric simplification. This involves reducing the complexity of geometries while maintaining sufficient precision for query purposes.

3. Spatial Partitioning:
   - Splitting large geospatial datasets into smaller partitions can significantly improve performance. Spatial partitioning allows the system to focus resources on the relevant area of the query, reducing the amount of data to be processed.

4. Efficient Use of Relational Database Indexes:
   - In relational database management systems, it is important to leverage traditional indexes in addition to spatial indexes. Optimizing spatial queries often involves a balance between specific indexes and traditional indexes.

5. Parallel Geoprocessing:
   - In cases of queries involving large volumes of data, the use of parallel geoprocessing techniques can distribute the workload among several cores or machines, thus speeding up query execution.

6. Use of Cache:

- Implementing spatial caches can store results of frequent queries, reducing the need to re-execute the same query repeatedly. This is especially useful in applications involving static or semi-static queries.

7. Spatial Algorithm Optimization:
- The choice of specific algorithms to perform spatial operations, such as intersections and unions, can significantly affect performance. Optimized algorithms can reduce computational complexity.

8. Performance Profile Analysis:
- Conducting performance profile analyzes helps identify bottlenecks and areas for improvement. Profiling tools can highlight which parts of the query consume the most resources and thus guide optimizations.

9. Incremental Index Update:
- In dynamic environments where geospatial data is frequently updated, implementing strategies to incrementally update spatial indices can be crucial to maintaining operational efficiency.

Optimizing spatial queries is not just a matter of improving response speed, but also managing resources efficiently. In large geospatial datasets, operational efficiency is vital to ensure the usefulness and viability of systems and applications. The strategies mentioned above, when applied carefully and considering the specific nature of the data and queries, can result in significant performance improvements.

Chapter 5: Importing and Exporting Geospatial Data

5.1. Geospatial Data Import

Importing geospatial data into database systems is a fundamental step towards incorporating geographic information into a structured storage environment. This process involves transferring geospatial datasets, such as maps, satellite images, geographic coordinates and geometries, to a spatial database management system (DBMS). Let's explore the import process and highlight some practical considerations:

Geospatial Data Import Process:

1. Choice of Data Format:
   - The first step is to choose the format of the geospatial data to be imported. Common formats include Shapefiles, GeoJSON, KML, and raster files like TIFF.

2. Database Schema Configuration:
   - Before importing, you must ensure that the database schema is configured to accommodate the geospatial data. This includes defining required tables, fields, and spatial indexes.

3. Choose Import Tool:
   - Several spatial DBMSs provide specific tools for importing geospatial data. Additionally, there are independent tools such as ogr2ogr and shp2pgsql that

make it easy to convert and import data into different formats.

4. Field Mapping:
 - During the import process, it is necessary to map the geospatial data fields to the corresponding fields in the database. This step ensures that the information matches correctly.

5. Projection Treatment:
 - Projection considerations are vital. It is important to ensure that the data is in the same projection or perform conversions when necessary. Consistency in projections is crucial for accurate spatial analysis.

6. Non-Spatial Data Handling:
 - In addition to geospatial data, there are often associated non-spatial attributes. These attributes must be considered and mapped appropriately to the corresponding fields in the database.

7. Validation and Cleaning:
 - Before importing, it is advisable to perform validation and cleaning checks on the data. This includes detecting and correcting invalid geometries, missing values, or any anomalies in the data.

8. Process Optimization:

- In large datasets, optimizing the import process is essential. This may include parallelizing operations or using spatial indexes to speed up data insertion.

9. Metadata Record:
  - Keeping records of metadata during import is a best practice. This includes information about the data source, import dates, and details about any transformations performed.

Practical Considerations:

- Scalability: Consider scalability of the import process to efficiently handle large volumes of geospatial data.

- Security: Ensure that data imports are carried out securely, avoiding potential vulnerabilities.

- Incremental Update: For dynamic datasets, implement strategies for incremental updates, minimizing redundancy in the import process.

- Standards and Compliance: Follow spatial standards and compliances, such as those defined by the OGC (Open Geospatial Consortium), to ensure data interoperability and consistency.

- Backup: Before carrying out the import, it is advisable to back up the database to avoid accidental data loss.

- Monitoring and Logging: Implement monitoring and logging mechanisms to track import progress and identify potential problems.

Importing geospatial data is a crucial stage in building robust geographic information systems. The success of this process not only depends on choosing the right tools, but also on careful attention to detail, from database configuration to validating imported data.

5.2. Geospatial Data Formats

Geospatial data is information that is associated with a specific location on Earth. To store and exchange this data efficiently, several formats have been developed, each with its specific characteristics and purposes. Below, I provide a conceptual look at some of the most common geospatial data formats, such as Shapefile, GeoJSON, and KML, highlighting how format choice can impact efficiency and interoperability.

1. Shapefile:
- Shapefile is a format developed by ESRI (Environmental Systems Research Institute) and is widely used in geographic information systems (GIS). It consists of several files that store different aspects of geospatial data, including geometries (points, lines, polygons) and associated attributes. Although widely adopted, Shapefile has some limitations, such as limited

support for 3D data and lack of direct support for non-geographic data.

2. GeoJSON:
- GeoJSON is a format based on JSON (JavaScript Object Notation) designed to represent geospatial data in a simple and lightweight way. It supports different types of geometries (points, lines, polygons) and associated attributes. GeoJSON's simplicity and readability make it popular for web applications and cross-platform interoperability. Its structure is easy to understand and is easily integrated with web technologies.

3. KML (Keyhole Markup Language):
- Developed by Keyhole (acquired by Google), KML is an XML format for representing geospatial data in three dimensions, commonly associated with Google Earth. It supports points, lines, polygons, images and 3D models. KML is suitable for visualization, but may not be as efficient as other formats in terms of file size for large datasets.

Impacts on Efficiency and Interoperability:

1. Storage Efficiency:
- The Shapefile format can generate relatively large files, especially for complex datasets, while GeoJSON, being text-based, tends to have a larger file size compared to binary formats like Shapefile. Storage

efficiency can impact data transfer and performance during read and write operations.

2. Online Transmission Efficiency:
- Choosing GeoJSON can be advantageous for online data transmission due to its lightweight structure and ease of integration with web technologies, being particularly useful in interactive and dynamic applications.

3. Interoperability:
- GeoJSON has been widely adopted for interoperability between different systems and platforms due to its text-based nature, which makes it easier to read and understand. Shapefile, as an ESRI proprietary format, may have interoperability limitations in environments that do not use ESRI products.

4. Support for Non-Spatial Attributes:
- The ability to support non-geographic data varies between formats. Shapefile is primarily aimed at geospatial data, while GeoJSON has more flexibility for including non-spatial attributes.

5. 3D Data Support:
- If representing data in three dimensions is a requirement, the KML format is a suitable choice as it is designed to work with three-dimensional data and is especially associated with Google Earth.

The choice of geospatial data format depends on the specific application requirements, considering factors such as storage efficiency, interoperability and support for specific functionalities, such as non-geographic or three-dimensional data. Each format has its place and is valuable in different contexts, and selection should be made based on the specific needs of the project or application in question.

5.3. Geospatial Data Conversion

Geospatial data conversion is a fundamental process that involves transforming geographic information from one format, coordinate system, or resolution to another. This practice is essential for interoperability between different systems, to guarantee data accuracy and to allow the efficient integration of geospatial information in different contexts. Let's explore the key aspects of this process and the associated importance:

1. Conversion between Formats:
   - Motivation: Different software and systems can use different geospatial data formats. Conversion between these formats is necessary to ensure that data can be read and interpreted correctly.
   - Example: Convert a dataset from Shapefile to GeoJSON to facilitate integration with a web application.

two. Coordinate Systems Transformation:

- Motivation: Geospatial data often uses different coordinate systems. Transformation between systems is crucial to ensure that locations are correctly represented in geographic space.

- Example: Convert coordinates from a geographic coordinate system (latitude, longitude) to a projected coordinate system (UTM).

3. Resolution Adjustment:

- Motivation: In some situations, it may be necessary to adjust the resolution of geospatial data to meet specific analysis, visualization, or storage requirements.

- Example: Reduce the resolution of a raster dataset to optimize performance in a web application.

4. Multisource Data Integration:

- Motivation: Geospatial data often comes from different sources with different formats and coordinates. Conversion is necessary to integrate and analyze data sets in a cohesive manner.

- Example: Integrate remote sensing data with registration data for more comprehensive analyses.

5. Harmonization for Spatial Analysis:

- Motivation: To perform meaningful spatial analysis, it is important that the data is in a format and coordinate system that allows coherent spatial operations.

- Example: Harmonize data from different sources to perform consistent buffer analysis.

Importance of Geospatial Data Conversion:

1. Interoperability:
   - Facilitates the integration of data from different sources and systems, allowing interoperability between different software and platforms.

2. Accuracy and Consistency:
   - Ensures data accuracy, ensuring that geospatial information is represented in a coherent and consistent way.

3. Significant Analysis:
   - Enables you to perform meaningful spatial analysis by adjusting data to formats and coordinate systems that are best suited for specific operations.

4. Efficient Visualization:
   - Facilitates efficient data visualization, especially when it comes to adjusting resolutions to optimize display in different contexts.

5. Urban Planning and Decision Making:
   - Plays a crucial role in sectors such as urban planning and decision-making, where the integration and analysis of geospatial data are fundamental.

6. Consolidation of Information:
   - Enables you to consolidate geospatial information from multiple sources to create comprehensive and cohesive datasets.

7. Adaptation to Specific Requirements:
  - Enables data adaptation to meet specific requirements of different applications, such as games, navigation systems, precision agriculture, among others.

Conversion of geospatial data is an essential practice for ensuring the usefulness and interoperability of geographic information in a variety of applications. The ability to transform data to meet specific requirements is crucial for accurate analysis, informed decision making, and efficient information integration in complex geoinformation environments.

5.4. Geospatial Data Export

Exporting geospatial data from a database system is an important process that allows geographic information to be used in different contexts, shared between systems, and analyzed externally. Let's explore the export process, how it is carried out, and highlight some common export formats and their practical applications:

Geospatial Data Export Process:

1. Data Selection:
  - The first step is to identify and select the geospatial data that will be exported. This may involve defining

selection criteria, such as geographic area, specific attributes, or any other relevant condition.

2. Output Format Setting:
    - Next, you need to choose the output format for the exported data. Different formats are suitable for different purposes, and the choice will depend on the specific user or application requirements.

3. Coordinate System Configuration:
    - If the data is in a specific coordinate system in the database, it may be necessary to configure the output coordinate system, especially if the data is exported for use in a different context.

4. Attribute Configuration:
    - It is possible to configure which attributes (fields) of the data will be exported. This allows you to customize the output to include only the relevant information.

5. Export Process:
    - The database system usually provides specific tools or commands to perform the export. This process may involve generating files or datasets that are ready to be used in other applications or systems.

Common Export Formats and Practical Applications:

1. Shapefile (.shp):
    - Practical Applications: Shapefile is a format widely used in geographic information systems (GIS) and is

suitable for storing geospatial data in the form of points, lines and polygons. It can be used in various GIS applications.

2. GeoJSON (.geojson):
   - Practical Applications: GeoJSON is a lightweight and easy-to-read text format, widely used in web applications. It is the common choice for exporting geospatial data for viewing on interactive maps on the internet.

3. KML (.kml):
   - Practical Applications: KML is often associated with Google Earth and is used to represent geospatial data in three dimensions. It is commonly used for three-dimensional and interactive visualizations.

4. CSV (Comma-Separated Values):
   - Practical Applications: The CSV format is simple and widely supported. It is useful for exporting tabular data associated with geographic locations, and is easy to integrate with spreadsheet and database software.

5. GPKG (Geopackage):
   - Practical Applications: Geopackage is a geospatial database format that can store both vector and raster data. It is useful when you want to maintain the original database structure, including spatial indexes and relationships.

6. TIFF (Tagged Image File Format):

- Practical Applications: The TIFF format is commonly used to export raster data, such as satellite images or topographic maps. It is widely supported in GIS software and image processing tools.

Importance of Exporting Geospatial Data:

1. Information Sharing:
    - Allows the sharing of geographic information between different users, organizations or systems.

2. Integration with Various Applications:
    - Facilitates the integration of geospatial data into diverse applications, from GIS systems to web visualization tools.

3. External Analysis:
    - Allows geospatial data to be analyzed externally in specific software environments, expanding analysis possibilities.

4. View and Presentation:
    - Facilitates the export of data to formats compatible with visualization tools, allowing the creation of maps and visual presentations.

5. Backup and Archiving:
    - Enables the creation of backup copies or archiving of geospatial data to preserve information over time.

Exporting geospatial data is a versatile and essential process that plays a crucial role in the efficient dissemination, sharing and analysis of geographic information. The choice of export format will depend on the specific needs of each case, considering practical applications and interoperability requirements.

5.5. Integration with Geographic Information Systems (GIS)

Integration between geospatial database systems (SGBD) and Geographic Information Systems (GIS) is essential to perform comprehensive analyzes and achieve effective visualizations of geographic data. These two types of systems play distinct but complementary roles in the management and analysis of geospatial information. Let's explore how this integration occurs and the associated benefits:

Integration between Geospatial Database Systems and GIS:

1. Efficient Geospatial Data Storage:
   - Geospatial DBMSs are designed to store and manage geospatial data efficiently, using spatial indexes to optimize information retrieval. Integration allows geospatial data to be stored in a structured way, ensuring integrity and retrieval efficiency.

2. Use of Specific Features:

- Geospatial DBMSs offer specific functionalities for manipulating spatial data, such as advanced spatial queries, topological operations and support for geographic coordinate systems. Integration allows you to leverage these specialized functionalities during data analysis.

3. Interoperability and Compatibility:

- The integration between geospatial DBMS and GIS facilitates interoperability and compatibility between different systems. Data stored in a geospatial DBMS can be easily imported and used in a GIS environment and vice versa, providing smooth integration.

4. Advanced Geospatial Analytics:

- The combination of spatial analysis functionalities of geospatial DBMS and GIS allows for advanced geospatial analysis. This includes identifying patterns, performing complex queries, and performing specialized spatial operations.

5. Data Visualization:

- GIS are designed to visualize and graphically represent geospatial data on maps. Integration with geospatial DBMS enables direct visualization of data stored in the database, facilitating interpretation and visual analysis.

6. Real-Time Update:

- Integration allows real-time updating of data between the geospatial DBMS and the GIS. This is especially crucial in dynamic environments where geospatial information is constantly evolving.

Integration Benefits:

1. Efficiency in Data Management:
    - Integration provides an efficient approach to managing large volumes of geospatial data, ensuring its availability and accessibility when needed.

2. Precise and Contextualized Analysis:
- The combination of geospatial data stored in DBMS with the analytical tools of a GIS allows for more precise and contextualized analyses, considering geographic location.

3. Informed Decision Making:
    - By integrating geospatial data, organizations can base their decisions on more complete and contextualized information, improving decision-making in areas such as urban planning, environmental management and public services.

4. Efficient Planning and Monitoring:
    - Integration facilitates efficient planning and continuous monitoring of specific geographic areas, enabling rapid response to significant changes or events.

5. Visualization Improvement:

- The integrated visualization of geospatial data in a GIS allows for an easier and faster understanding of patterns and trends, contributing to more effective communication.

Integration between geospatial database systems and Geographic Information Systems is critical to obtaining maximum value and insights from geospatial data. This synergy allows for more efficient management, more accurate analysis and effective visualization, contributing significantly to informed decision-making in various sectors.

Chapter 6: Geocoding and Geoprocessing

6.1. Data Geocoding

Data geocoding is a process by which non-spatial information, such as addresses, place names, or other location descriptors, is converted into geographic coordinates, allowing the precise location of these elements in a geospatial context. This process is fundamental for linking non-spatial data to a geographic position on the Earth's surface, facilitating spatial analysis and visualization on maps.

Here are the main aspects of data geocoding:

1. Transformation of Descriptors into Coordinates:
   - Geocoding involves transforming location descriptors, such as addresses or place names, into geographic coordinates that represent the specific position on Earth.

2. Use of Geographic Databases:
   - To perform geocoding, geographic databases are often used that contain information about the relationship between location descriptors and geographic coordinates. These databases may be maintained by geocoding services such as Google Maps or by organizations that maintain precise location information.

3. Geocoding Methods:

- There are several geocoding methods, and the choice of method may depend on the nature of the data and the desired accuracy. Some common methods include address-based geocoding, where the address is translated into coordinates, and reverse geocoding, where coordinates are used to find an address.

4. Geocoding Accuracy:
- Geocoding accuracy may vary depending on the quality of the data used in the process and the resolution of the methods used. Geocoding can be highly accurate in well-mapped urban areas, but may be less accurate in rural regions or in locations with less detailed geocoding information.

5. Practical Applications:
- Geocoding is fundamental in several applications, including navigation systems, company location, demographic data analysis, asset management and many other areas where geographic location is relevant.

6. Advantages for Spatial Analysis:
- By geocoding data, you can integrate non-spatial information into existing geospatial datasets. This enriches spatial analysis, enabling patterns to be identified, informed decision-making and map visualization.

Practical example:
Imagine a dataset containing addresses of a company's customers. Geocoding this dataset would

convert these addresses into geographic coordinates (latitude and longitude), enabling the creation of maps that show the geographic distribution of customers. This information could be used to optimize delivery routes, identify areas of highest customer concentration and support localized marketing strategies.

Geocoding is an essential process that transforms non-spatial information into geospatial data, paving the way for meaningful spatial analysis and a deeper understanding of the relationship between data and location on the Earth's surface.

6.2. Geoprocessing

Geoprocessing: A Conceptual View

Geoprocessing is a discipline that encompasses a set of techniques, methods and technologies aimed at the collection, storage, analysis, interpretation and representation of geospatial data. This interdisciplinary field uses a systematic approach to deal with information related to geographic location, allowing a deeper and more efficient understanding of Earth's space and its interactions.

Main Geoprocessing Components:

1. Geospatial Data Acquisition:

- The geoprocessing process begins with the acquisition of geospatial data, which may include remote sensing information, GPS data, digital maps, satellite images, among others. The accuracy and quality of this data is crucial for accurate geospatial analysis.

2. Storage in Geographic Databases:
- Geospatial data is often stored in geographic databases, which are optimized to handle spatial information. These databases not only store the geometry of elements, but also support spatial queries and operations.

3. Spatial Analysis:
- Spatial analysis is the core of geoprocessing, involving the application of operations and techniques to investigate patterns, relationships and trends within geospatial data. This may include proximity analysis, pattern analysis, surface modeling, among other methods.

4. Geospatial Modeling:
- The use of spatial models is an essential part of geoprocessing. Geospatial models can simulate real-world phenomena and predict future scenarios, contributing to strategic planning across multiple disciplines.

5. Visualization and Cartographic Representation:
- Geoprocessing includes techniques for effective visualization of geospatial data. This ranges from the

creation of conventional maps to representation in three-dimensional or interactive environments, allowing clear and accessible communication of information.

Applications of Geoprocessing in Various Areas:

1. Urban Planning:
   - Geoprocessing is widely used in urban planning to analyze growth patterns, identify risk-prone areas, optimize land use and support decisions related to infrastructure and urban mobility.

2. Environmental Management:
   - In environmental management, geoprocessing is crucial for monitoring environmental changes, assessing the health of ecosystems, identifying priority conservation areas and managing natural resources sustainably.

3. Precision Agriculture:
   - In the agricultural sector, geoprocessing is applied to optimize production through the analysis of data on soils, topography, climate and vegetation. This allows for the implementation of more efficient and sustainable agricultural practices.

4. Water Resources Management:
   - In water resources management, geoprocessing is used to model river basins, analyze precipitation patterns, identify aquifer recharge areas and manage the sustainable use of water.

5. Public Health:

- In the health sector, geoprocessing is applied to map the distribution of diseases, analyze environmental factors that can affect public health and optimize the location of health services.

6. Logistics and Transport:

- In the logistics and transport sector, geoprocessing is used to optimize routes, analyze traffic patterns, plan road infrastructure and monitor the movement of goods.

Geoprocessing plays a central role in the analysis and interpretation of geospatial data, offering a powerful approach to understanding complex interactions in the geographic environment. Its application in various areas contributes to informed decision-making, strategic planning and the promotion of sustainable practices in an increasingly interconnected world.

6.3. Network Analysis and Routing

Network Analysis and Routing in Geoprocessing: An Informative Approach

Network analysis and routing in geoprocessing is a specialized area that focuses on understanding and optimizing connectivity between geographic locations, allowing efficient modeling of displacements and the identification of more effective routes. These techniques play a crucial role in various practical applications such as logistics, transportation, urban planning and resource management.

Main Components of Network Analysis in Geoprocessing:

1. Network Modeling:
- The first step in network analysis is to create a modeled representation of geographic infrastructure as a network. This involves defining elements such as roads, rails, rivers, or other travel elements, as well as the nodes that connect these elements.

2. Cost Allocation:
- Each segment of the network is assigned a cost, which can represent distance, travel time, financial cost, or any other relevant metric. This cost assignment is fundamental to determining route efficiency.

3. Routing Analysis:
- Routing analysis aims to identify the most efficient route between two or more points in the network. This

may involve minimizing distances, travel times or costs associated with the route.

4. Connectivity Identification:
- Network analysis also allows the identification of connectivity between different parts of the network. This is crucial to understanding how geographic locations are interconnected and how changes in one part of the network can affect other areas.

Practical Applications of Network Analysis in Geoprocessing:

1. Logistics and Distribution:
- Logistics companies use network analysis to optimize delivery routes, minimizing transport costs and delivery time. This is vital to ensure efficiency in supply chains.

2. Urban Planning:
- In urban planning, network analysis is applied to optimize the layout of infrastructures, such as roads and public transport, ensuring efficient and accessible distribution for the population.

3. Traffic Management:
- Network analysis is used in traffic management systems to predict congestion, optimize traffic lights and improve traffic flow in urban areas.

4. Emergency Services:

- In emergency services, such as firefighters and ambulances, network analysis is crucial for finding quick and efficient routes to the scene of the incident, optimizing emergency response.

5. Public Transport Planning:
- Public transport agencies use network analysis to optimize routes, timetables and station locations, improving the efficiency of public transport.

Routing in Geoprocessing:

1. Routing Algorithms:
- Various algorithms are employed to determine efficient routes in a network. Dijkstra, A* and Floyd-Warshall algorithms are common examples used to find the shortest or most efficient path between two points.

2. Dynamic Considerations:
- In addition to static routing, network analysis in geoprocessing also considers dynamic aspects, such as real-time traffic, weather conditions and unforeseen events that can affect route conditions.

3. Routing Customization:
- Advanced routing systems allow customization of routes based on user preferences, such as avoiding tolls, choosing more scenic routes, or avoiding congested areas.

Benefits of Network Analysis and Routing:

1. Operational Efficiency:
   - Optimizes operational efficiency in various sectors, reducing costs and improving the use of resources.

2. Informed Decision Making:
   - Facilitates informed decision-making in logistics, transportation and urban planning based on accurate and efficient analysis.

3. Improvement in Resource Distribution:
   - Contributes to a more efficient distribution of resources, minimizing redundancies and ensuring effective use of available infrastructure.

4. Adaptation to Variable Conditions:
   - The ability to consider changing conditions in real time allows for effective adaptation to changing traffic conditions, events or other dynamic variables.

Network and routing analysis in geoprocessing plays a crucial role in optimizing displacements and understanding connectivity in a geographic context. Its practical applications are wide and varied, contributing to more efficient management and informed decision-making in different sectors of society.

6.4. Geocoding Applications

Practical Applications of Geocoding in Different Sectors:

Geocoding, which involves assigning geographic coordinates to non-spatial data, plays a key role in many industries, driving efficiency and providing valuable insights. Here are some of the practical applications in different industries:

1. Logistics and Supply Chain:
- Route Optimization: Logistics companies use geocoding to optimize delivery routes, minimizing distances and transport times, resulting in more efficient operations and reduced costs.
- Real-Time Tracking: The ability to geocode delivery points in real-time allows for accurate tracking of goods throughout the entire supply chain.

two. Marketing and Advertising:
- Market Segmentation: Geocoding is used to segment markets based on location, allowing for more targeted and personalized marketing campaigns for specific audiences in certain regions.
- Customer Location Analysis: Retailers can use geocoded data to understand the geographic distribution of their customers, adapt marketing strategies and decide on the location of new stores.

3. Public Services and Urban Planning:

- Urban Planning: Urban planning bodies employ geocoding to understand demographic distribution, identify areas of growth and optimize urban development.

- Waste Management: Geocoding is used to optimize waste collection routes, improving efficiency in urban waste management.

4. Health and Social Services:

- Distribution of Health Resources: Geocoding assists in the efficient allocation of health resources, identifying areas with the greatest need and ensuring accessibility of services.

- Epidemiological Monitoring: Assigning coordinates to disease case addresses allows for effective monitoring of outbreaks and helps implement preventive measures.

5. Real Estate and Construction:

- Real Estate Market Analysis: In the real estate sector, geocoding is used for market analysis, identifying price and demand trends in different regions.

- Asset Location: In construction, geocoding helps in the precise location of assets, such as public service networks, facilitating the planning and execution of projects.

6. Agriculture and Environment:

- Agricultural Monitoring: Farmers use geocoding to monitor variables such as soil conditions and climate, optimizing agricultural practices and increasing productivity.

- Environmental Management: Assigning coordinates to critical locations, such as conservation areas and water resources, allows for effective environmental management and informed decision-making about preservation.

7. Energy Sector:
- Infrastructure Maintenance: Energy companies use geocoding to optimize infrastructure maintenance, identifying critical locations and acting preventively to avoid failures.
- Location of Energy Assets: Assigning coordinates to assets such as transmission towers and stations allows for more efficient management of these resources.

8. Insurance:
- Risk Assessment: Insurance companies apply geocoding to assess risks based on location, determining insurance premiums and risk management strategies.
- Claims Management: Geocoding facilitates claims management, allowing a quick and efficient response to events such as natural disasters.

General Benefits:
- Informed Decision Making: Geocoding provides a solid foundation for informed decision making, allowing businesses and organizations to better understand the geographic distribution of data and improve their strategies.

- Operational Efficiency: By assigning coordinates to non-spatial data, operations become more efficient, resulting in time and resource savings.
- Improvement in Customer Experience: Sectors such as retail and services can use geocoding to improve the customer experience, offering personalized services based on location.

Geocoding is a versatile and essential tool that transcends industries, driving efficiency across multiple operations and contributing significantly to strategic decision-making in a geographic context.

6.5. Challenges in Geocoding

Challenges in Geocoding: Accuracy, Update and Privacy

Geocoding, despite being a powerful tool for assigning geographic coordinates to non-spatial data, faces a series of challenges that can affect the accuracy of information, the updating of databases and raise concerns related to privacy. Here are some of the main challenges:

1. Data Accuracy:
- Accuracy is a critical challenge in geocoding. Errors can arise due to inconsistencies in input data, missing details in addresses, or fluctuations in the quality of geospatial data sources. Inadequate precision can result

in incorrect locations, directly impacting the reliability of analysis and decision making.

two. Database Update:

   - Keeping geocoded databases up to date is a constant challenge. Changes in urban infrastructure, new developments, address updates and changes in geography can make data outdated. This requires continuous efforts to ensure that geocoded information is aligned with the reality of the environment.

3. Spatial Resolution and Interpolation:

   - Spatial resolution is a challenge, especially in areas with varying population densities. In urban regions, where address density is high, geocoding may be more accurate, while in rural or undeveloped areas, accuracy may decrease. Interpolation, i.e. estimating a location between known data, may be necessary, but presents challenges when there is not enough information.

4. Privacy Issues:

   - Geocoding raises significant privacy concerns. When assigning geographic coordinates to data, there is a risk of identifying sensitive information, such as home addresses. This is particularly critical in sectors such as healthcare and social services, where patient or citizen privacy is a priority.

5. Quality of Data Sources:

   - The quality of geospatial data sources is crucial to geocoding accuracy. Depending on the region, sources may vary in terms of availability, reliability and detail. Using low-quality data sources can compromise the accuracy and reliability of geocoded information.

6. Dynamic Changes in the Environment:
   - Dynamic changes in the environment, such as new road construction, street closures, real estate development, and changes in urban infrastructure, pose challenges to keeping geocoding up to date. Databases must monitor these changes in a timely manner.

7. Legal and Consent Issues:
   - Using data for geocoding often requires legal and consent considerations. Ensuring that data is obtained and used ethically and legally is a challenge, especially when dealing with customer, patient or citizen data.

Approaches to Overcoming Challenges:

1. Continuous Validation: Implementing continuous data validation processes, including regular accuracy checks, is essential to ensure the reliability of geocoded information.

2. Dynamic Data Integration: Using dynamic data sources and systems that can be updated in real time is crucial to dealing with constant changes in the environment.

3. Strict Privacy Policies: Develop and adhere to strict privacy policies, ensuring that geocoding is performed ethically and in compliance with privacy regulations.

4. Geocoding Algorithm Improvements: Develop and improve geocoding algorithms to deal with different challenges such as varying spatial resolution and accurate interpolation in data-sparse areas.

5. Transparency and Consent: Establish transparency in geocoding practices by obtaining appropriate consent from individuals when necessary and ensuring information is used ethically.

Addressing these challenges is essential to ensuring that geocoding is a reliable and effective tool across industries, enabling organizations to make informed decisions and optimize their operations in an ethical and efficient manner.

Chapter 7: Security in Geospatial Databases

7.1. Security Considerations

Security Considerations in Geospatial Databases: Protecting Geographic Location Sensitive Information

Security in geospatial databases is of paramount importance as these systems deal with sensitive information related to geographic location, which can include personal data, confidential business data and critical infrastructure information. Effective protection of this data requires the implementation of specific security measures, integrated with general database security principles. Here are some essential considerations:

1. Access control:
   - General Principle: Limiting access to data to only authorized users is fundamental to the security of any database.
   - Application in Geospatial Databases: Ensure that only authorized users can view or manipulate sensitive geospatial information, especially that related to personal location data.

two. Data Encryption:
   - General Principle: Encryption protects confidential data, making it unintelligible to unauthorized users.
   - Application in Geospatial Databases: Use encryption to protect geospatial data during storage and transmission, especially when dealing with personal or strategic information.

3. Suspicious Activity Monitoring:

- General Principle: Monitoring and recording activities in the database helps in early detection of unauthorized access or suspicious activities.

- Application in Geospatial Databases: Implement monitoring systems that alert about unusual access patterns or unauthorized access attempts to geospatial data.

4. Authentication and Authorization:

- General Principle: Authentication verifies the user's identity, while authorization controls access permissions based on that identity.

- Application in Geospatial Databases: Establish robust authentication and authorization procedures to ensure that only authorized users can interact with geospatial data.

5. Updates and Patches:

- General Principle: Keeping your database software updated with the latest fixes and security patches is vital.

- Application in Geospatial Databases: Ensure that any software used to manage geospatial data is updated to mitigate known vulnerabilities.

6. Backup and Recovery:

- General Principle: Performing regular backups is crucial for quick recovery in case of data loss due to failure or attack.

- Application in Geospatial Databases: Implement robust backup policies, considering the importance of geospatial data, and regularly test recovery procedures.

7. Data Anonymization:
   - General Principle: Anonymizing sensitive data can reduce the risk of involuntary exposure.
   - Application in Geospatial Databases: When storing or sharing sensitive geospatial data, consider anonymization techniques to protect individuals' privacy.

8. Physical and Environmental Security:
   - General Principle: Physically protecting servers and ensuring a secure environment around them is crucial.
   - Application in Geospatial Databases: Consider the physical security of servers that store geospatial data to prevent unauthorized access or damage.

9. Data Retention Policies:
   - General Principle: Setting clear policies on data retention and secure deletion prevents unnecessary storage.
   - Application in Geospatial Databases: Establish specific policies for geospatial data, especially when dealing with temporary or sensitive information.

10. Regulatory Compliance:
    - General Principle: Complying with relevant safety regulations and standards is essential.
    - Application in Geospatial Databases: Stay informed about specific regulations related to geospatial privacy

and ensure compliance with standards such as GDPR (General Data Protection Regulation) in specific regions.

Integrating these security considerations into geospatial databases is crucial to ensure data integrity, confidentiality and availability, as well as to comply with legal requirements related to privacy and information security. A holistic approach, considering technical, procedural and people aspects, is necessary to create a robust security posture.

7.2. Access control

Access Control in Geospatial Databases: Protecting Location Sensitive Data

Access control plays a fundamental role in the security of geospatial databases, as it regulates and limits who can access, modify and delete sensitive data related to geographic location. This approach is essential to ensure the confidentiality, integrity and availability of geospatial data. Let's explore how access control operates in this context and which strategies are effective.

Role of Access Control:

1. Confidentiality: Access control ensures that only authorized users are allowed to view sensitive location

information. This is crucial to protecting personal, business and strategic data stored in geospatial databases.

2. Integrity: Limiting who can modify or add data is essential to maintaining the integrity of geospatial data. The insertion of incorrect or malicious information that could distort analysis or location-based decisions is avoided.

3. Availability: Ensuring that only authorized users can access the geospatial database contributes to data availability. This protects against unauthorized access that could result in interruptions or unavailability of services.

Efficient Access Control Strategies:

1. Strong Authentication: Implement strong authentication methods, such as multi-factor authentication (MFA), to verify users' identities before granting access to geospatial data.

2. Granular Authorization: Establish granular permissions, assigning different levels of access based on users' roles and responsibilities. For example, an analyst might have permission to view data, while an administrator has permission to modify it.

3. Group Policies: Organizing users into groups with specific permissions makes access control

administration easier. This is especially useful in environments where different teams have different access needs.

4. Audit Log: Keeping detailed records of activities, such as who accessed, modified or deleted data, contributes to security. Audit logs enable rapid detection of suspicious activity and can be essential for security investigations.

5. Periodic Reviews: Carrying out periodic reviews of access permissions is crucial. As users' responsibilities change, their permissions must also be adjusted to ensure that only authorized people have access.

6. Role-Based Control (RBAC): Implementing a role-based access control model allows for the efficient assignment of permissions based on the roles played by users, simplifying administration and ensuring consistency.

7. Segregation of Duties: Avoiding excessive concentration of powers is important. Segregation of duties involves dividing functions so that no one person has complete control over a process.

8. Encryption of Sensitive Data: Using encryption to protect sensitive data, both at rest and in transit, adds an additional layer of security, ensuring that even if unauthorized access occurs, the data remains protected.

9. Physical Access Restriction: In addition to logical control, ensuring that only authorized personnel have physical access to servers that store geospatial data is vital to global security.

10. Updates and Training: Staying up to date with security best practices and providing ongoing training to users and system administrators is critical to ensuring access control strategies remain effective over time.

Access control in geospatial databases plays a crucial role in protecting sensitive location data. Effective strategies must range from authentication to encryption, ensuring a comprehensive approach to information security in a geospatial context.

7.3. Audit and Tracking

Audit and Tracking in Geospatial Databases: Monitoring and Securing Critical Operations

Auditing and tracking geospatial databases are fundamental practices that play a crucial role in monitoring activities, identifying potential threats, and maintaining detailed records of operations performed on the data. These practices are essential to ensure the integrity, confidentiality and availability of geospatial data. Let's explore the concepts underlying these practices.

Audit on Geospatial Databases:

1. Activity Monitoring:
   - Auditing involves continuous monitoring of activities in the geospatial database. Each action, such as accessing, modifying or deleting data, is recorded for later analysis.

2. Anomaly Identification:
   - Through auditing, it is possible to identify unusual access patterns or suspicious activities. This includes multiple login attempts, massive data changes, or any activity that could indicate a security threat.

3. Compliance and Regulations:
   - Auditing is essential to ensure compliance with specific regulations such as GDPR (General Data Protection Regulation) in specific regions. Audit records serve as evidence of compliance.

4. Investigation and Incident Response:
   - In case of security incidents, audit logs play a crucial role in the investigation. They help reconstruct events, identify the source of the threat, and determine the extent of the impact.

Tracking in Geospatial Databases:

1. Detailed Operations Record:
   - Tracking involves creating detailed records of each operation performed on geospatial data. This includes information such as who performed the operation, when it was performed, and what data was affected.

2. Change History:
   - Tracking allows you to create a history of changes to data. This is crucial for understanding how data has evolved over time, making it easier to analyze trends and roll back to previous versions if necessary.

3. Users' Responsibility:
   - By tracking each operation down to the user level, the system creates an environment of accountability. This encourages the adoption of safe practices, knowing that each user's actions are recorded.

4. Integrity Guarantee:
   - Tracking contributes to ensuring data integrity. If unauthorized modifications occur, tracking records allow you to identify when and how those modifications were made.

The Joint Importance of Auditing and Tracking:

1. Prevention and Early Detection:
   - The combination of auditing and tracking is effective in preventing unauthorized access and early detection of suspicious activity.

2. Informed Decision Making:
   - Detailed audit and tracking logs provide critical information for informed decision making. This is especially important in security incident situations or when analyzing significant changes to geospatial data.

3. Compliance and Responsibility:
   - Both practices are essential to ensure compliance with security regulations and standards and to establish a culture of accountability among users and system administrators.

4. Continuous Improvement:
   - By regularly reviewing audit and tracking logs, organizations can identify areas for improvement in database security and implement corrective measures.

   Auditing and tracking are fundamental pillars of security in geospatial databases. These practices provide a comprehensive view of activities in the system, enabling rapid response to incidents, ensuring compliance, and ensuring data integrity over time.

7.4. Sensitive Data Protection

Protecting Sensitive Data in Geospatial Databases: Safeguarding Privacy and Security

Protecting sensitive data in geospatial databases is a primary concern, especially given the nature of the location-related information. Ensuring the privacy and security of this data involves implementing robust measures to minimize risks. Below are specific strategies and considerations related to protecting sensitive data in geospatial environments.

1. Anonymization and Pseudonymization:
   - Strategy: Replace personally identifiable information with identifiers not directly related to the individual's identity.
   - Objective: Minimize the risk of personal identification while still enabling valuable geospatial analysis.

two. Granular Access Control:
   - Strategy: Implement granular access control, assigning specific permissions based on user needs.
   - Objective: Ensure that only authorized users have access to sensitive location data, limiting exposure.

3. Data Encryption:
   - Strategy: Use encryption to protect sensitive data at rest and in transit.
   - Purpose: Add a layer of security to prevent unauthorized access even if data is compromised.

4. Data Minimization:
   - Strategy: Collect and store only the geospatial data necessary for the specific purpose, avoiding excessive retention.

- Objective: Reduce exposure and potential impact in the event of a data breach.

5. Audit and Tracking:
   - Strategy: Implement detailed auditing and tracking to monitor all activities in the geospatial database.
   - Purpose: To quickly identify and respond to unauthorized access, improper modification or suspicious activity.

6. Informed consent:
   - Strategy: Obtain informed consent from users before collecting and processing sensitive location data.
   - Purpose: Ensure compliance with privacy regulations and demonstrate transparency in data collection practices.

7. Data Retention Policies:
   - Strategy: Establish clear policies on the retention and secure disposal of sensitive data.
   - Objective: Avoid unnecessary maintenance of information and reduce the risk of exposure.

8. User Training:
   - Strategy: Provide regular training to users on security practices and the importance of protecting sensitive data.
   - Objective: Create a culture of awareness that minimizes human errors that could lead to security breaches.

9. Segregation of Duties:
- Strategy: Separate responsibilities to ensure that no person has unrestricted access to sensitive data.
- Objective: Prevent potential abuse or unauthorized access through the controlled distribution of responsibilities.

10. Regulatory Compliance:
- Strategy: Stay up to date with geospatial privacy regulations such as GDPR and ensure full compliance.
- Objective: Avoid legal penalties and demonstrate commitment to protecting privacy.

Effective implementation of these strategies not only protects the privacy of individuals but also strengthens the overall security of the geospatial database. When considering the sensitive nature of location data, the approach to protection must be holistic, encompassing technical, procedural and user awareness aspects.

7.5. Backup and Recovery

Backup and Recovery in Geospatial Databases: Ensuring Continuity and Resilience

The importance of backup and recovery in geospatial databases is fundamental to ensuring operational continuity and data resilience, especially in the face of adverse events. These practices play a crucial role in protecting against data loss, system failures, natural disasters, and cyber threats. Let's explore why these strategies are essential and some of the associated best practices.

Importance of Backup and Recovery:

1. Resilience against Hardware and Software Failures:
   - In a geospatial environment, where data integrity is crucial, hardware or software failures can result in significant losses. Backup ensures quick recovery of this data, minimizing operational impact.

2. Protection against Natural Disasters:
   - Natural disasters, such as earthquakes, floods or fires, can threaten physical and digital infrastructure. Backup, stored in secure locations off-site, provides an additional layer of protection against complete data loss.

3. Cyber Threat Mitigation:
   - With the increase in cyber threats, attacks like ransomware can compromise critical data. Backup becomes an essential tool to restore data after malware removal, minimizing the impact of such incidents.

4. Continuous Availability Guarantee:
   - Fast and efficient recovery through backups ensures continuous availability of geospatial data. This is crucial,

especially in scenarios where disruptions could have serious implications, such as in emergency services or navigation.

Best Practices in Backup and Recovery:

1. Regular Backup Schedule:
   - Establishing a regular schedule for running backups is essential. This ensures that recent changes to data are captured, reducing potential loss in the event of a failure.

2. Secure and Redundant Storage:
   - Storing backups in secure, redundant locations is crucial. This can include secondary servers, cloud services, and off-site locations to protect against disasters.

3. Recovery Tests:
   - Performing regular recovery tests is a vital practice. This verifies the effectiveness of backups and ensures that the recovery process is smooth and fast when needed.

4. Historical Versions:
   - Maintaining historical versions of backups allows data recovery to specific moments in time, useful in cases of data corruption that may not be immediately detected.

5. Detailed Documentation:

- Documenting backup and recovery procedures in detail is essential to facilitate effective implementation in emergency situations. This is crucial, especially in complex geospatial environments.

6. Backups Encryption:
   - Encrypting backups ensures data security during storage and transfer. This is crucial, especially when dealing with sensitive geospatial data.

7. Process Automation:
   - Automating the backup process reduces the risk of human error and ensures that backups are performed according to the established schedule.

8. Retention Policies:
   - Establish clear backup retention policies, determining how long backups will be kept. This helps you efficiently manage storage and meet regulatory requirements.

Effectively implementing backup and recovery practices is critical to preserving the integrity, availability, and resilience of geospatial data. These strategies not only protect against accidental losses, but also strengthen response capabilities in emergency scenarios.

Chapter 8: Integrating Geospatial Data with Applications

8.1. API e Web Services

APIs and Web Services: Facilitating Geospatial Data Integration

APIs (Application Programming Interfaces) and Web Services play a crucial role in integrating geospatial data with applications, enabling efficient communication between systems and facilitating the sharing of geographic information. Let's explore how these technologies work and why they are essential in this context.

1. Definition of APIs and Web Services:

- APIs: An API is a set of rules and protocols that allows one application to communicate with another. In essence, it is a bridge that allows interaction between different systems or software components.

- Web Services: They are a specific category of APIs that use World Wide Web standards to facilitate communication between systems distributed over the internet. Web Services can be accessed via HTTP (Hypertext Transfer Protocol) and are generally implemented using standards such as SOAP (Simple Object Access Protocol) or REST (Representational State Transfer).

two. Role of APIs and Web Services in Geospatial Data:

- Efficient Communication:
  - APIs and Web Services provide an efficient way for systems to exchange geospatial data. Applications can make specific requests to obtain geographic information from other sources, or even send geospatial data to be processed externally.

- Communication Standardization:
  - By using standards such as REST or SOAP, Web Services offer a standardized form of communication. This facilitates interoperability between different systems, regardless of the programming languages or platforms used.

- Remote Data Access:
  - APIs and Web Services enable access to remote geospatial data. This is particularly useful in scenarios where data is distributed across different servers or systems, allowing applications to access geographic information without the need to have all the data locally.

- Integration with External Systems:
  - Organizations often use a variety of systems to manage geospatial data. APIs and Web Services facilitate the integration of these systems, allowing them to work together harmoniously.

- Real-Time Update:
  - The use of Web Services facilitates real-time updating of geospatial data. This is essential in applications that

require accurate and up-to-date geographic information, such as navigation services or real-time monitoring.

3. Examples of Use in Geospatial Data:

- Online Map Services:
  - Many online map services, such as Google Maps or OpenStreetMap, offer APIs that allow developers to embed interactive maps into their own applications.

- Geocoding and Routing:
  - Geocoding and routing APIs, like those provided by the Google Maps API, allow developers to integrate location and navigation functionality into their applications.

- Integration with GIS Systems (Geographic Information Systems):
  - APIs and Web Services are widely used to integrate GIS systems, allowing geospatial data to be shared between different GIS platforms.

4. Additional benefits:

- Scalability:
  - APIs and Web Services offer scalability, allowing systems to easily grow and adapt as demands for geospatial data increase.

- Ease of Maintenance:

- Updates to individual systems can be made without negatively affecting other systems that integrate through APIs. This simplifies the maintenance and evolution of applications.

- Promotion of Innovation:
  - By making APIs available, organizations encourage innovation, allowing external developers to create new applications and services that use geospatial data.

In summary, APIs and Web Services play a central role in the efficient integration of geospatial data into diverse applications. These technologies not only facilitate communication between systems, but also promote interoperability and support the creation of more robust and innovative applications in the geospatial domain.

8.2. Integration with Mobile Apps

Integration of Geospatial Data in Mobile Applications: Enriching Experiences and Facilitating Decision Making

The integration of geospatial data into mobile applications represents a revolution in digital experiences, allowing users to access relevant contextual information based on their geographic location. This synergy between geospatial data and mobile applications not only enriches the user experience but also offers innovative and practical functionalities. We will explore how this integration occurs and provide practical examples.

How Integration Happens:

1. Geospatial APIs for Developers:
   - Mobile app developers can leverage geospatial APIs, such as Google Maps API or Mapbox API, to incorporate mapping, geocoding, and routing functionality into their apps.

2. Use of Device Location Services:
   - Modern mobile devices are equipped with GPS receivers and other location sensors. Applications can use these services to obtain the user's current location and present relevant information based on that position.

3. Integration with External Data:
   - In addition to standard map services, applications can integrate with external geospatial databases to obtain specific information about points of interest, recommended routes or environmental data.

Practical examples:

1. Navigation and Routing:
   - Navigation apps like Google Maps use geospatial data to provide accurate routes and real-time traffic information, allowing users to make informed decisions about their journeys.

2. Location-Based Augmented Reality:
   - Applications that use location-based augmented reality offer immersive experiences by overlaying geospatial information onto the physical environment. This could include details about tourist attractions, restaurants or historical information.

3. Delivery and Logistics Applications:
   - Delivery companies use geospatial data to optimize delivery routes, track vehicles in real time, and provide users with accurate information about the status of their orders.

4. Urban Planning Applications:
   - Applications developed for urban planning can provide interactive visualizations of the urban environment, incorporating data on building zones, traffic planning and green areas.

5. Health and Wellbeing Apps:
   - Fitness apps that integrate geospatial data can track running routes, provide information about hiking trails, and even warn about polluted areas.

6. Location-Based Marketing:
   - Companies use geospatial data to personalize offers and ads based on the user's location, providing a more relevant and targeted experience.

Integration Benefits:

1. Contextual Relevance:
   - Geospatial data integration allows applications to provide contextually relevant information, adapting to the user's specific location.

2. Informed Decision Making:
   - Users can make more informed decisions based on geographic information, such as choosing the fastest route, discovering points of interest, or receiving relevant alerts.

3. Innovative Experiences:
   - Combining geospatial data with mobile features such as motion sensors and cameras opens up space for innovative experiences such as augmented reality navigation or location-based gaming.

4. Operational Efficiency:
   - Industries such as logistics and delivery services can optimize operations, reduce delivery times and improve overall efficiency based on real-time geospatial data.

Ultimately, the integration of geospatial data into mobile applications represents a significant evolution in the way we interact with technology in our everyday lives. This synergy offers not only practicality and efficiency, but also opens doors to the creation of innovative and contextually rich digital experiences.

8.3. Integration with Planning Systems

Integration of Geospatial Data with Planning Systems: Optimizing Strategic Processes

Integrating geospatial data with planning systems is a strategic approach that offers significant advantages in several sectors, such as urban, logistics and environmental planning. This synergy allows for a more holistic and contextualized understanding of data, improving operational efficiency and enabling more informed decision-making. Let's explore the concept of this integration and highlight specific use cases.

The Concept of Integration:

The integration of geospatial data with planning systems refers to the combination of geographic information with the processes and decisions inherent to strategic planning. It involves the collection, analysis and interpretation of relevant geospatial data to enrich the context of specific planning systems.

Integration Advantages:

1. Holistic View:
   - The incorporation of geospatial data offers a comprehensive and visual view of the environment under analysis. This is particularly valuable in urban planning, where visualization of physical space is key.

2. Informed Decision Making:
   - Integration allows decision makers to consider crucial geographic factors. In logistics, for example, the location of warehouses and distribution centers can be optimized based on geospatial data.

3. Operational Efficiency:
   - In logistics planning, integration with geospatial data helps optimize delivery routes, reducing transit times and improving operational efficiency.

4. Sustainable Urban Planning:
   - In urban planning, geospatial data is crucial for assessing urban expansion, identifying areas prone to natural disasters, and planning efficient land use to promote sustainability.

5. Environmental Monitoring:
   - In environmental planning systems, geospatial data allow monitoring changes in environmental conditions, assessing biodiversity and planning interventions for preservation.

Specific Use Cases:

1. Urban Planning:
   - In urban expansion, the integration of geospatial data helps identify areas suitable for development,

considering factors such as accessibility, existing infrastructure and potential environmental impacts.

2. Logistics and Supply Chain:
   - In logistics, integration with geospatial data facilitates route management, locating strategic warehouses and reducing costs associated with transport.

3. Precision Agriculture:
   - In agriculture, geospatial data is used to optimize the use of resources, such as water and fertilizers, based on the specific characteristics of each cultivated area.

4. Public Service Planning:
   - When planning public services, such as water and energy networks, the integration of geospatial data facilitates the identification of areas that require improvements or maintenance.

5. Disaster Management:
   - In natural disaster situations, the integration of geospatial data allows for a faster and more effective response, identifying affected areas and optimizing the targeting of resources.

The integration of geospatial data with planning systems is a fundamental step towards optimizing strategic processes in various areas. By incorporating geographic information, planning systems gain a more complete and contextualized dimension, providing tangible benefits in terms of efficiency, sustainability and informed decision-making.

8.4. Geospatial Data Visualization

The Importance of Geospatial Data Visualization: Improved Understanding and Decision Making

Geospatial data visualization plays a crucial role in interpreting and effectively communicating geographic information. By transforming complex data into understandable visual representations, it facilitates analysis, promotes deeper insights, and is essential for supporting informed decision-making. Let's explore the importance of visualization and the techniques/tools used to present geospatial data effectively.

Importance of Visualization:

1. Spatial Contextualization:
   - Visualization provides an instant understanding of the spatial context of the data. This is crucial for areas such as urban planning, environmental management and logistics, where geographic location is fundamental for decision-making.

2. Identification of Patterns and Trends:
   - Charts, maps and 3D visualizations enable quick identification of patterns and trends in geospatial data.

This makes it easier to uncover valuable insights that might otherwise be missed in purely tabular datasets.

3. Effective Communication:

- Clear visualizations are essential for communicating complex geospatial information to diverse audiences. They simplify complicated concepts, making data accessible and understandable to a wider audience.

4. Informed Decision Making:

- Effective visualization empowers decision makers to understand the spatial implications of data. This is crucial in areas such as emergency management, where speed in decision-making is vital.

5. Interactive Exploration:

- Interactive visualization tools allow users to explore geospatial data dynamically. This promotes deeper understanding as users can focus on specific areas of interest.

Visualization Techniques and Tools:

1. Maps:

- Maps are a fundamental form of geospatial visualization. They can range from simple maps to interactive maps that incorporate additional layers of information, such as population density, weather patterns, or infrastructure.

2. Spatial Graphs:

- Charts that incorporate geographic information, such as bar charts or spatial scatterplots, can provide insights into the distribution of data across different regions.

3. 3D View:
- 3D environments are effective for representing geospatial information in three dimensions. This is valuable in sectors such as architecture, urban planning and geology.

4. Geographic Infographics:
- Infographics are visual representations that can include maps, graphs and icons to communicate geospatial information in a concise and attractive way.

5. Augmented Reality (AR):
- AR integrates geospatial data into the physical environment, providing an immersive experience. This is valuable in fields such as tourism, education and urban design.

Importance in Data Interpretation:

1. Identification of Spatial Relations:
- Visualizations make it easier to identify spatial relationships between different datasets, allowing for deeper analysis.

2. Anomaly Detection:

- By visualizing spatial patterns, it is easier to detect anomalies or areas that stand out, indicating the need for further investigation.

3. Distribution Understanding:
- Visualization helps understand the spatial distribution of phenomena, from population concentration to climate patterns.

4. Effective Communication:
- By presenting geospatial data in a visual way, communication is improved, facilitating information sharing and collaboration between teams.

5. Temporal Analysis Support:
- Temporal graphs and geospatial animations allow analysis of changes over time, providing valuable insights into seasonal patterns or evolutions.

Geospatial data visualization is essential for extracting meaning and value from complex information. It not only enhances understanding, but also plays a key role in effective communication and informed decision-making across a variety of industries.

8.5. Integration Case Studies

Successful Case Studies in Geospatial Data Integration: Efficiency, Innovative Decisions and Technological Impact

The integration of geospatial data has been fundamental in a variety of applications, providing significant benefits in terms of operational efficiency, decision-making and technological innovation. Below are some successful case studies that illustrate how this integration has driven notable advancements across different industries.

1. Uber: Real-Time Route Optimization

* Context:
   - Uber uses geospatial data extensively to optimize travel routes in real time. This not only improves the user experience, but also reduces travel time and optimizes vehicle allocation.

* Benefits:
   - Operational Efficiency: Geospatial data integration allows Uber to dynamically optimize routes based on real-time traffic, resulting in faster, more efficient trips.

   - Informed Decision Making: Continuous analysis of geospatial data enables informed decisions about expansion strategies, identifying areas of high demand and growth opportunities.

2. Esri: ArcGIS for Sustainable Urban Planning

* Context:
    - Esri, a company specializing in geographic information systems (GIS), has implemented ArcGIS in sustainable urban planning projects in several cities.

* Benefits:
    - Operational Efficiency: Integration allows a detailed analysis of the urban environment, optimizing land use, identifying areas suitable for green projects and facilitating infrastructure planning.

    - Decision Making for Sustainability: Geospatial visualizations provide critical data for decisions aimed at sustainability, such as creating green areas, waste management and public transport planning.

3. NASA Worldview: Global Climate Monitoring

* Context:
    - NASA Worldview is a platform that integrates geospatial data for global climate monitoring. It aggregates information from satellites and provides real-time views.

* Benefits:
    - Technological Innovation: The integration of advanced geospatial data allows researchers, scientists and the general public to monitor global climate events in real time, contributing to the understanding and mitigation of climate change.

4. Zillow: Geospatial Visualization for Real Estate

* Context:
- Zillow, a real estate marketplace platform, uses geospatial data to provide detailed property information, including pricing, sales history, and local demographics.

* Benefits:
- Efficiency in Real Estate Search: Integration of geospatial data makes it easier for users to efficiently search for properties based on specific criteria such as location, price and neighborhood characteristics.

- Informed Decision Making: With detailed information and geospatial views, buyers and sellers have a solid foundation for making informed decisions in the real estate market.

5. World Bank: Epidemic Monitoring

* Context:
- The World Bank uses geospatial data integration to monitor epidemics at a global level. This involves analyzing health data, population movements and environmental conditions.

* Benefits:
- Rapid Response to Epidemics: Integration of geospatial data enables faster response to disease outbreaks, facilitating the efficient allocation of

healthcare resources and the development of containment strategies.

- Location-Based Decision Making: With geospatial visualizations, health authorities can identify risk areas, coordinate vaccination efforts, and implement preventive measures more effectively.

These case studies highlight how geospatial data integration not only optimizes operational processes, but also drives technological innovation and supports informed decision-making across a variety of industries, demonstrating the significant impact of this interdisciplinary approach.

Chapter 9: Big Data and Geospatial Data

9.1. Geospatial Data in Big Data Environments

Geospatial Data in Big Data Environments: Integration for Scalable and Innovative Analysis

Geospatial data, due to its complex and voluminous nature, finds a favorable environment for efficient analysis and management in Big Data systems. Integrating this data into Big Data environments provides opportunities for deeper insights, informed decision-making, and innovation in a variety of areas. Let's explore how geospatial data fits into Big Data environments and the importance of this integration.

Nature of Large-Scale Geospatial Data:

1. Significant Volume:
   - Geospatial data often represents vast sets of information, including location information, maps, satellite images, and temporal data. The considerable volume of this data can quickly reach massive dimensions.

2. Spatial and Temporal Complexity:
   - The spatial complexity of geospatial data lies in the three-dimensional representation of the real world. Furthermore, much of this data is dynamic, varying over time. This adds a temporal dimension, making them

more challenging and, at the same time, more information-rich.

3. Variety of Formats:
- Geospatial data can take many formats, including vector data, raster data, remote sensing data, and more. Integrating and analyzing these diverse formats requires flexible and adaptable approaches.

Management in Big Data Systems:

1. Distributed Storage:
- Big Data environments, such as Hadoop Distributed File System (HDFS), enable distributed storage of large-scale geospatial data. This approach facilitates horizontal scalability, making it possible to deal with large volumes of data efficiently.

2. Parallel Processing:
- Big Data systems, such as Apache Spark, offer parallel processing capabilities. This is crucial for simultaneously analyzing large geospatial data sets, significantly reducing processing times.

3. Specific Tools:
- Tools and libraries specific to geospatial data, such as GeoSpark and GeoMesa, were developed to operate effectively in Big Data environments. They offer advanced functionality for spatial queries and analysis.

4. Integration with Machine Learning Frameworks:

- Big Data environments often integrate machine learning frameworks, such as TensorFlow or Apache Flink, enabling advanced predictive analysis on geospatial data.

5. Distributed Visualization:
- Big Data systems can also be integrated with distributed visualization tools, such as Apache Superset or Tableau, to graphically represent the results of geospatial analyses.

Importance of Integration:

1. Scalable Analytics:
- The integration of geospatial data in Big Data environments allows for analysis at scale, enabling the efficient processing of large volumes of data and the execution of complex spatial queries in real time.

2. Informed Decision Making:
- The ability to analyze geospatial data in conjunction with other data sources in Big Data environments expands understanding of context, enabling more informed decision-making in various sectors, such as logistics, urban planning and environmental sciences.

3. Technological Innovation:
- The integration of geospatial data in Big Data environments drives technological innovation, enabling the creation of advanced solutions such as accurate

navigation systems, real-time environmental risk analysis and large-scale route optimization.

4. Efficiency in Temporal Analysis:
   - Big Data environments facilitate the analysis of geospatial data over time, enabling the identification of temporal patterns, seasonal trends and dynamic analyzes for sectors such as agriculture, climate monitoring and disaster management.

The integration of geospatial data into Big Data environments represents a powerful synergy, enabling scalable analytics, informed decision-making and technological innovations. This not only expands analytical capabilities but also drives transformation across multiple industries that rely heavily on geographic information.

9.2. Large-Scale Data Processing

Large-Scale Geospatial Data Processing: Distributed Strategies and Innovative Technologies

Large-scale geospatial data processing involves applying distributed techniques to handle large volumes of geographic data efficiently. As the amount of geospatial data continues to grow, it becomes imperative to employ scalable approaches. We will explore how distributed processing techniques are applied in this context and highlight commonly used technologies.

Challenges in Geospatial Data Processing:

1. Significant Volume:
   - Geospatial data often represents vast sets of information, including maps, satellite images, and temporal data. The significant volume of this data can overwhelm conventional processing systems.

2. Spatial and Temporal Complexity:
   - The spatial and temporal complexity of geospatial data increases the processing load. The three-dimensional representation of the real world and the temporal dynamics of data require specialized approaches.

3. Need for Complex Analysis:
   - Geospatial analytics often involve complex operations such as spatial queries, spatial data joining, and proximity analysis, which can be computationally intensive.

Distributed Processing Techniques:

1. Divide and Conquer (MapReduce):
   - The MapReduce technique divides a complex task into smaller tasks, called "map" and "reduce", which can be distributed among several processing nodes. It is effective for parallelizable operations such as image

processing and extracting information from large geospatial datasets.

2. Batch and Real-Time Processing:
   - Distributed systems can process geospatial data in batches or in real time. While batch operations are efficient for historical analysis, real-time processing is crucial for applications that require immediate responses, such as real-time monitoring.

3. Distributed Spatial Indexing:
   - Distributed spatial indexing, such as the use of R-tree indexes in distributed systems, facilitates efficient spatial queries. This technique is essential for operations such as searching for nearby points or region-based filtering.

4. Parallelism in Spatial Queries:
   - The ability to distribute spatial queries across multiple processing instances enables the simultaneous execution of complex operations on large data sets. This is fundamental for operations such as density analysis and spatial clustering.

Commonly Used Technologies:

1. Apache Hadoop:
   - Hadoop is a framework that supports the implementation of the MapReduce model. It is effective

for processing large volumes of geospatial data in batches.

2. Apache Spark:
    - Spark offers a faster, more flexible approach to distributed processing, enabling interactive analytics and real-time operations. It is particularly useful for complex operations on geospatial data.

3. GeoSpark:
    - GeoSpark is a Spark extension designed specifically for geospatial processing. It provides efficient geospatial operations and is integrated with the Spark ecosystem.

4. HBase:
    - HBase is a distributed NoSQL database that can be used to store geospatial data. It offers fast access to indexed spatial data.

5. Apache Flink:
    - Flink is a real-time processing platform that supports complex analytics and spatial queries on continuous data streams.

Importance and Impact:

1. Operational Efficiency:

- Distributed processing significantly improves operational efficiency by enabling fast and accurate analysis of large geospatial data sets.

2. Real-Time Analysis:
- Real-time distributed processing enables real-time monitoring, rapid response to events and continuous analysis.

3. Scalable Applications:
- Distributed processing techniques make geospatial applications scalable, supporting continuous growth of data and users.

4. Technological Innovation:
- These approaches are fundamental to technological innovation

9.3. Distributed Storage

Distributed Storage of Geospatial Data in Big Data Environments: Scalability and Efficiency

Distributed storage of geospatial data in Big Data environments is a fundamental approach to dealing with the complexity and massive volume of this data. This distributed strategy not only offers scalability, but also provides greater efficiency in managing large sets of geographic information. Let's explore the concept of distributed storage and the technologies commonly used in this context.

Distributed Storage Concept:

Distributed storage is a paradigm in which data is distributed among multiple nodes in a system, rather than being centralized in a single location. Each node contains a portion of the data, and distribution is managed in a coordinated manner to ensure data integrity and accessibility. This not only contributes to scalability but also provides redundancy and fault tolerance.

Contributions to Scalability:

1. Load Distribution:
   - By distributing geospatial data among several nodes, the storage and processing load is distributed equitably. This avoids bottlenecks and allows the system to efficiently meet increasing demands.

2. Parallelism:
   - Distributed architecture allows parallel execution of operations on different parts of the data. This is crucial for performing complex spatial queries on large geospatial datasets, significantly improving performance.

3. Horizontal Expansion:

- As the amount of geospatial data grows, it is possible to add new nodes to the system to expand storage and processing capacity. This approach offers horizontal scalability, crucial in Big Data environments.

Commonly Employed Distributed Storage Technologies:

1. Hadoop Distributed File System (HDFS):
- HDFS is a core solution in the Hadoop ecosystem. It divides data into blocks distributed across multiple nodes, providing high availability and fault tolerance.

2. Cassandra:
- Cassandra is a distributed NoSQL database, effective for storing geospatial data. Provides linear scalability and failure resilience.

3. Amazon S3 (Simple Storage Service):
- S3 is a distributed storage service from AWS, enabling the efficient and secure storage of large volumes of geospatial data.

4. Google Cloud Storage:
- Similar to S3, Google Cloud Storage is a solution distributed on the Google Cloud platform, offering advanced storage and retrieval features.

5. HBase:
- HBase is a distributed NoSQL database integrated with Hadoop. Provides a scalable framework for storing geospatial data in distributed tables.

Advantages of Distributed Storage for Geospatial Data:

1. Redundancy and Fault Tolerance:
   - Data distribution provides redundancy, reducing the risk of losing information in the event of a failure in one of the nodes.

2. Efficient Recovery:
   - Distribution allows efficient data recovery even in failure situations, ensuring high availability.

3. Continuous Evolution:
   - The addition of new nodes allows the continuous evolution of the system, adapting to the growth of geospatial data.

4. Optimized Performance:
   - Parallel and distributed operations improve overall performance, especially in complex spatial queries.

Distributed storage of geospatial data in Big Data environments represents an essential approach to addressing the challenges inherent to the complexity and volume of this data. These solutions not only provide scalability, but also ensure operational efficiency and high availability in a context where large geospatial data sets are the norm.

9.4. Geospatial Data Analysis in Big Data

Geospatial Data Analysis in Big Data Environments: Advanced Techniques for Meaningful Insights

Geospatial data analysis in Big Data environments involves applying advanced techniques to extract meaningful insights from large sets of geographic data. We will explore the main techniques, algorithms and specific tools used in this context.

1. Distributed Processing:
- In Big Data environments, distributed processing is fundamental. Tools like Apache Spark are widely used to process large volumes of geospatial data efficiently, enabling complex analyzes and the extraction of relevant information.

two. Spatial Pattern Analysis:
- Spatial pattern analysis algorithms, such as Getis-Ord Gi* (G for Getis and O for Ord), are applied to identify spatial clusters of high or low incidence of events. This technique is valuable in areas such as epidemiology, urban planning and environmental monitoring.

3. Geoanalytics:
- Platforms specialized in geoanalytics, such as GeoMesa, allow the analysis of large sets of geospatial data in real time. This is crucial in scenarios like traffic

monitoring, where real-time analysis of location data is essential.

4. Machine Learning Espacial:
  - Machine learning algorithms adapted for geospatial data, such as Support Vector Machines (SVM) and Random Forest, are applied to tasks such as classifying satellite images, predicting movement patterns and identifying geospatial anomalies.

5. MapReduce for Spatial Queries:
  - The MapReduce approach, popularized by Hadoop, is applied to spatial queries on large data sets. This enables efficient parallelization of complex spatial operations, improving performance.

6. Spatial-Temporal Analytics:
  - In many cases, the temporal dimension is crucial in the analysis of geospatial data. Spatiotemporal analysis techniques, such as the use of spatiotemporal OLAP cubes, are applied to understand patterns that evolve over time.

7. Interactive View:
  - Interactive visualization tools such as Tableau and Power BI are integrated with Big Data platforms to provide an intuitive graphical representation of geospatial data. This makes it easier to quickly interpret patterns and trends.

8. Geospatial Network Analysis:

- Network analysis algorithms, such as Dijkstra's algorithm for routing, are employed to understand connectivity in geographic environments. This analysis is valuable in logistics, transportation and urban planning.

9. Geolocated Sentiment Analysis:
- In data coming from social networks or media sources, geolocated sentiment analysis is applied to understand people's perception of specific locations. This is useful in marketing and making decisions based on venue reputation.

10. Space Simulation:
- Spatial simulation algorithms are applied to predict the future behavior of complex geospatial phenomena such as urban growth, regional climate change and the spread of diseases.

Geospatial data analysis in Big Data environments is a constantly evolving field, driven by the combination of advanced spatial analysis techniques, machine learning and distributed processing. The ability to extract meaningful insights from large geographic data sets is essential for informed decision-making in sectors such as urban planning, logistics, healthcare and the environment.

9.5. Challenges and Opportunities

Challenges and Opportunities in Integrating Geospatial Data with Big Data

The integration of geospatial data with Big Data offers a series of challenges and opportunities, reflecting the complexity inherent in analyzing large sets of geographic data. We will explore these aspects, highlighting the difficulties faced and the potential innovations that may arise.

Challenges:

1. Complexity in Spatial Analysis:
   - The complexity of geospatial data is increased when integrated with massive sets of Big Data. Spatial analysis requires advanced algorithms and specialized techniques to deal with the dimensionality and heterogeneity of these data.

2. Need for Specialized Tools:
   - Analyzing geospatial data in Big Data environments requires specialized tools that can efficiently handle complex operations and large-scale spatial queries. The scarcity of generic tools can be an obstacle.

3. Dimensionality Management:
   - Geospatial data often has multiple dimensions, including spatial and temporal coordinates. Managing

and analyzing this dimensionality effectively is challenging, especially when combined with large volumes of data.

4. Integration of Data from Different Sources:
    - Geospatial data integration often involves fusing information from different sources, such as remote sensors, mobile devices and social networks. Aligning and harmonizing this data can be complicated due to different formats and standards.

5. Privacy and Security:
    - Geospatial data often contains sensitive information related to specific locations. Ensuring the privacy and security of this data, especially in shared Big Data environments, is a crucial concern.

Opportunities:

1. Discoveries at Scale:
    - Integrating geospatial data with Big Data offers the opportunity to make discoveries at scale, revealing patterns and correlations that would not be noticeable in smaller data sets. This is especially relevant in scientific research, urban planning and environmental monitoring.

2. Innovation in Spatial Analysis:
    - The challenges associated with large-scale spatial analysis drive innovation in algorithms and analysis techniques. New methods are developed to deal with

the complexity of data, paving the way for significant advances in understanding geographic phenomena.

3. Location-Informed Decision Making:
   - Efficient integration of geospatial data with Big Data provides a robust foundation for location-informed decision making. This is particularly valuable in sectors such as logistics, precision agriculture and natural resource management.

4. Real-Time Applications:
   - The ability to analyze real-time geospatial data in Big Data environments opens up opportunities for dynamic applications such as real-time traffic monitoring, disaster response and route optimization.

5. Holistic Understanding of Context:
   - The integration of geospatial data with Big Data allows for a more holistic understanding of the spatial context. This is critical to understanding the complex interactions between geographic variables and other data, resulting in deeper insights.

Integrating geospatial data with Big Data is a challenging field, but the opportunities for large-scale innovation and discovery are significant. While we face technical and management challenges, the rewards include a deeper understanding of the world around us and the ability to make more informed and effective decisions. The search for creative solutions and the continuous development of specialized tools are essential to unlock the full potential of this integration.

Chapter 10: Geospatial Data Applications and Industries

10.1. Precision agriculture

Precision Agriculture: The Role of Geospatial Data in Agricultural Optimization

Precision agriculture is a modern approach that uses geospatial data to optimize agricultural practices, providing significant benefits in terms of efficiency, productivity and sustainability. Here are some fundamental ways geospatial data is applied in precision agriculture:

1. Soil Mapping:
   - Geospatial data is employed to map soil characteristics, including texture, nutrients and moisture levels. This information is crucial for understanding soil variability in an agricultural area, allowing segmentation into specific management zones.

two. Remote sensing:
   - Remote sensing technologies such as satellite imagery and drones provide high-resolution geospatial data on plant health, growth patterns and potential problems. This allows for early detection of pests, diseases and nutritional deficiencies.

3. Climate Monitoring:

- Geospatial climate data, such as temperature, humidity and rainfall patterns, are fundamental in precision agriculture. Real-time monitoring of these variables helps farmers adjust their planting, watering and harvesting schedules according to specific weather conditions.

4. Variable Rate Farming:

- Based on geospatial data, farmers can implement variable rate agriculture, adjusting the application of inputs (such as fertilizers and agrochemicals) according to the specific characteristics of each part of the field. This not only reduces costs, but also minimizes environmental impacts.

5. Global Positioning Systems (GPS):

- The integration of global positioning systems (GPS) in precision agriculture allows accurate mapping of agricultural activities such as planting, spraying and harvesting. This contributes to the detailed recording of operations and the creation of productivity maps.

6. Automation and Robotics:

- Using geospatial data, autonomous systems and agricultural robots can be programmed to perform specific tasks, such as sowing or harvesting in specific areas of the field. This not only increases efficiency but also reduces dependence on human labor.

7. Topographic Monitoring:

- Geospatial data assists in topographic monitoring of the terrain, helping farmers understand variation in elevation, drainage and other important characteristics. This information is crucial for planning irrigation systems and preventing problems such as erosion.

Benefits of Precision Agriculture with Geospatial Data:

1. Resource Optimization:

- Precision agriculture allows for the efficient allocation of resources, such as water and agricultural inputs, reducing waste.

2. Increased Efficiency:

- By adapting agricultural practices to the specific conditions of each area, farmers are able to achieve greater production efficiency.

3. Cost Reduction:

- The precise use of inputs results in a significant reduction in operating costs, improving profitability.

4. Minimization of Environmental Impacts:

- Precision agriculture contributes to more sustainable agricultural practices, minimizing the overapplication of inputs and reducing adverse environmental impacts.

5. Informed Decision Making:

- Geospatial data empowers farmers to make informed decisions, taking into account spatial variability across their land.

Precision agriculture, driven by geospatial data, represents an innovative approach that not only increases agricultural efficiency but also promotes sustainability and resilience in the sector. This technological integration is transforming the way farmers manage their land, providing both economic and environmental benefits.

10.2. Natural Resource Management

Natural Resource Management: The Fundamental Role of Geospatial Data

Natural resource management is a crucial challenge, and geospatial data plays an essential role in this process. This information offers a comprehensive view of ecosystems, biodiversity and water resources, enabling more informed and sustainable decision-making. Let's explore how geospatial data is applied to natural resource management.

1. Ecosystem Mapping:
- Geospatial data is used to map and monitor ecosystems, identifying areas of forests, grasslands, wetlands and other types of natural habitats. This is

crucial for understanding the geographic distribution of ecosystems and assessing their conservation status.

two. Biodiversity Monitoring:
   - Information on biodiversity, including the distribution of plant and animal species, is mapped using geospatial data. This facilitates the monitoring of populations, identification of areas of high biodiversity and assessment of the impact of human activities on species.

3. Conservation of Protected Areas:
   - Geospatial data is fundamental for the management of protected areas, such as national parks and nature reserves. Accurately mapping these areas helps monitor illegal activities, plan conservation strategies, and evaluate the success of conservation initiatives.

4. Sustainable Land Use:
   - Sustainable land management is supported by geospatial data that provides information on current land use, vegetation cover changes and desertification processes. This data guides sustainable agricultural practices and prevents soil degradation.

5. Water Resources Monitoring:
   - Geospatial data is used to monitor the distribution and quality of water resources, including rivers, lakes and aquifers. This is crucial for sustainable water management, identifying areas prone to scarcity and implementing conservation practices.

6. Environmental Risk Analysis:
    - Geospatial mapping is vital for analyzing environmental risks such as landslides, forest fires and floods. This information helps to identify vulnerable areas and implement preventive measures.

7. Land Use Planning:
    - Geospatial data is crucial in land use planning, allowing the identification of suitable areas for urban development, agriculture and preservation. This approach aims to balance human needs with the conservation of natural ecosystems.

Benefits of Using Geospatial Data in Natural Resource Management:

1. Informed Decision Making:
    - Geospatial data provides a solid basis for informed decision-making, allowing natural resource managers to understand the complexity of the environment and its interactions.

2. Conservation Efficiency:
    - The conservation of natural areas is optimized with geospatial data, allowing the efficient allocation of resources to the most critical areas in terms of biodiversity and ecosystems.

3. Rapid Response to Environmental Emergencies:

- Continuous monitoring through geospatial data facilitates rapid response to environmental emergencies, minimizing damage in cases of natural disasters.

4. Community Engagement:
- Sharing geospatial data promotes community engagement, allowing communities to actively participate in the management of their local natural resources.

5. Environmental Impact Assessment:
- Projects and human activities that impact the environment can be accurately assessed using geospatial data, helping to mitigate negative impacts.

The application of geospatial data in natural resource management is essential to promote sustainability, biodiversity conservation and the efficient use of resources. This evidence-based approach significantly contributes to balancing human needs and preserving ecosystems.

10.3. Transportation and logistics

The Transformative Impact of Geospatial Data on the Transportation and Logistics Sector

The transportation and logistics sector is undergoing a revolution driven by geospatial data, providing a smarter, more efficient approach to managing operations. This information, related to routes, traffic and location, has a significant impact on all stages of the logistics chain, from planning to final delivery. Here are some key aspects of geospatial data's impact on this crucial sector:

1. Routing and Route Planning:
   - Geospatial data allows for optimized vehicle routing, considering variables such as distance, travel time, traffic conditions and even location-specific information such as height and weight restrictions.

two. Supply Chain Optimization:
   - The detailed view of geospatial data allows the optimization of the supply chain, from origin to final destination. This includes efficient supplier selection, strategically located distribution centers and optimal modes of transportation.

3. Real-Time Asset Monitoring:
   - Tracking systems based on geospatial data enable real-time monitoring of vehicles, goods and assets throughout the entire logistics chain. This improves visibility and responsiveness to unforeseen events.

4. Efficient Fleet Management:
   - Geospatial data is fundamental for efficient fleet management. They allow for precise maintenance

scheduling, vehicle performance monitoring and route optimization to minimize operating costs.

5. Demand and Stock Forecast:
    - Geospatial data analysis enables a better understanding of demand in different regions, allowing the anticipation of seasonal peaks and the adaptation of stock to meet the specific needs of each location.

6. Urban Traffic Management:
    - Real-time data on traffic and road conditions is crucial for efficient transportation management in urban areas. This includes identifying alternative routes in case of congestion.

7. Last Mile Planning:
    - Last mile optimization, the final phase of customer delivery, is enhanced by geospatial data. This includes choosing strategic delivery points and efficiently scheduling vehicles to minimize wait times.

8. Operational Efficiency Analysis:
    - Geospatial data enables comprehensive analysis of operational efficiency. This includes evaluating transit times, bottlenecks in the supply chain, and identifying opportunities for improvement.

Tangible Benefits of Using Geospatial Data in the Industry:

1. Operating Cost Reduction:

- Efficient routing, optimized fleet management and demand forecasting help reduce operational costs.

2. Increased Efficiency:
   - Intelligent use of geospatial data results in more efficient operations, from storage to final delivery.

3. Improvement in Customer Experience:
   - On-time delivery, real-time information and the ability to adapt to customer preferences significantly improve the customer experience.

4. Sustainability:
   - Route optimization and efficient asset management contribute to more sustainable practices, reducing carbon emissions.

5. Quick Response to Changes:
   - Real-time data enables rapid response to unexpected events, minimizing supply chain disruptions.

The incorporation of geospatial data in the transport and logistics sector represents a paradigm shift, driving efficiency, sustainability and responsiveness in a globalized and dynamic market. This is a clear example of how technology can fundamentally transform traditional industries, delivering tangible benefits to both businesses and consumers.

10.4. Urbanism and Urban Planning

The Transformative Role of Geospatial Data in Urbanism and Urban Planning

Geospatial data plays a fundamental role in urbanism and urban planning, providing valuable information about the geography and dynamics of cities. This data not only facilitates understanding of the urban environment, but also plays a crucial role in the sustainable development of cities. Here are some ways geospatial data impacts urbanism:

1. Mapping and Land Use Analysis:
   - Geospatial data allows precise mapping of urban land use. This includes identifying residential, commercial, industrial and green areas. Land use analysis helps urban planners understand the specific characteristics and needs of each region.

two. Infrastructure Planning:
   - The location of critical infrastructure such as roads, bridges, schools, hospitals and parks is improved by geospatial data analysis. This information is essential for planning new infrastructures and efficiently maintaining existing ones.

3. Population Density and Demography:
   - Geospatial data helps in mapping population density and demographic characteristics of different urban

areas. This information is crucial for understanding population distribution and planning services and resources equitably.

4. Risk Assessment and Urban Resilience:
   - The identification of risk areas, such as areas susceptible to floods, earthquakes or other natural disasters, is improved by geospatial analysis. This contributes to planning risk mitigation measures and increasing urban resilience.

5. Transport and Urban Mobility:
   - Geospatial data analysis is crucial for planning public transport systems, parking strategies, cycle routes and walking paths. This contributes to more efficient and sustainable urban mobility.

6. Green Zones and Public Spaces:
   - Geospatial data helps identify suitable areas for parks, squares and other green areas. These spaces are essential for the well-being of the community and to promote a high quality of life.

7. Environmental Impact Assessment:
   - Geospatial analysis is used to assess the environmental impact of urban projects. This includes identifying sensitive areas, preserving urban ecosystems and promoting sustainable construction practices.

Tangible Benefits of Using Geospatial Data in Urban Planning:

1. Sustainable Development:
   - The efficient use of geospatial data contributes to sustainable development, allowing urban planners to consider present needs without compromising future ones.

2. Efficiency in Decision Making:
   - Geospatial data offers a complete view of the urban environment, allowing decision makers to make informed choices to optimize space and resources.

3. Social Inclusion:
   - Analysis of population distribution and the specific needs of each area contributes to inclusive planning, ensuring that all segments of society benefit from urban resources.

4. Urban Resilience:
   - Identifying risks and implementing resilience measures based on geospatial data makes cities more prepared to face environmental and social challenges.

5. Improvement in Quality of Life:
   - Urbanism based on geospatial data aims to improve the quality of life, creating urban environments that are

greener, more accessible and adapted to the needs of the community.

Geospatial data is an invaluable tool in urban planning, empowering planners to create more efficient, sustainable and livable cities. The integration of this data into urban decisions not only optimizes the use of space, but also contributes to the development of more equitable and resilient communities.

10.5. Health and Environmental Monitoring

The Transformation of Health and Environmental Monitoring through Geospatial Data

Geospatial data plays a vital role in promoting public health and environmental monitoring, providing crucial insights into the complex interplay between the environment and human health. Here is how this data is innovatively applied in these fields:

1. Disease Pattern Mapping:
   - Geospatial data is used to map disease patterns, identifying areas with a higher prevalence of certain health conditions. This helps in efficient allocation of resources and planning specific interventions.

two. Epidemiological monitoring:

- Epidemiological surveillance benefits enormously from geospatial data. Identifying disease outbreaks, tracking cases, and understanding the geographic spread of infectious diseases are enhanced by spatial analyses.

3. Air Quality Monitoring:
- Geospatial sensors monitor air quality in specific locations, providing information on pollutant levels. These data are crucial for assessing the impact of air pollution on respiratory health and for developing mitigation strategies.

4. Identification of Environmental Risk Factors:
- Geospatial data helps identify environmental risk factors, such as exposure to toxic substances or proximity to sources of pollution. This is essential for preventing environmentally related diseases.

5. Healthcare Facilities Planning:
- Geospatial analysis is fundamental for the strategic planning of healthcare facilities. This includes identifying underserved areas, properly sizing hospitals and clinics, and efficiently allocating resources.

6. Response to Disasters and Public Health Emergencies:
- In situations of natural disasters or public health emergencies, geospatial data facilitates rapid and coordinated response. They help identify affected areas and distribute resources efficiently.

7. Disease Vector Monitoring:

- The location of disease vectors, such as mosquitoes that transmit tropical diseases, is monitored using geospatial data. This is vital to implementing effective disease control strategies.

8. Assessment of Social Determinants of Health:

- Geospatial analysis helps in the assessment of social determinants of health, such as access to healthy food, housing conditions and socioeconomic levels. These factors have a direct impact on the health of the population.

Concrete Benefits of Applying Geospatial Data to Health and Environmental Monitoring:

1. Precise Interventions:

- Mapping disease patterns allows for more precise interventions, directing resources to areas that need them most.

2. Prevention of Environmental Diseases:

- The identification of environmental risk factors contributes to the prevention of environmentally related diseases.

3. Informed Decision Making:

- Healthcare professionals can make more informed decisions based on geospatial data, improving the effectiveness of interventions.

4. Rapid Response to Disease Outbreak:
   - Real-time epidemiological surveillance facilitates rapid response to disease outbreaks, containing their spread.

5. Strategic Public Health Planning:
   - Geospatial analysis contributes to strategic planning of healthcare services, including the optimal location of medical facilities.

6. Sustainable Monitoring:
   - Sustainable environmental monitoring, including air quality, promotes healthier and more resilient communities.

The application of geospatial data in health and environmental monitoring not only enhances understanding of the complex links between environment and health, but also empowers communities to take proactive steps to improve quality of life and prevent disease. This innovative approach is shaping the future of public health and environmental monitoring.

Chapter 11: Maintaining and Updating Geospatial Data

11.1. Geospatial Data Lifecycle

Geospatial Data Lifecycle: Maintaining Accuracy Over Time

The geospatial data lifecycle comprises several phases, from initial collection to eventual data obsolescence. Understanding and managing this cycle is crucial to ensuring data remains accurate, relevant and reliable over time. Let's explore the main phases of this cycle:

1. Data collect:
    - Description: The first phase involves collecting geospatial data. This may include information obtained through satellites, ground-based sensors, field surveys, or other sources.
    - Importance: The accuracy and quality of the data in this phase directly influence the reliability of all subsequent phases.

two. Processing and Storage:
    - Description: Collected data is processed to remove errors, standardize formats and then stored in geospatial database systems.

- Importance: Proper processing and efficient storage ensure that data is ready for later analysis and retrieval.

3. Analysis and Visualization:
- Description: In this phase, geospatial data is analyzed to extract meaningful information. This may involve creating maps, identifying patterns, or complex analyses.
- Importance: Analysis and visualization provide valuable insights for decision-making and understanding the geographic environment.

4. Sharing and Distribution:
- Description: The analyzed data is shared internally or externally, often through online platforms, APIs or geoprocessing services.
- Importance: Efficient sharing is vital for collaboration, research and broad use of data.

5. Update and Maintenance:
- Description: Geospatial data is subject to change over time due to environmental, urban or other changes. Regular updates are required to ensure continued accuracy.
- Importance: Keeping data up to date is essential to avoid obsolescence and provide relevant information.

6. Archiving and Preservation:
- Description: As data ages or is replaced by newer information, it can be archived for historical reference. Proper preservation ensures future access.

- Importance: Some data may have historical value or be necessary to comply with regulations, justifying their preservation.

7. Obsolescence and Ethical Disposal:
   - Description: Eventually, data may become obsolete due to significant changes in the environment, outdated collection methods, or other reasons. In these cases, ethical disposal is necessary.
   - Importance: Avoiding the use of obsolete data is essential for informed decision making and error prevention.

General considerations:
- Standards and Metadata:
   - The application of standards and appropriate use of metadata throughout the entire lifecycle of geospatial data contributes to interoperability, understanding and traceability.

- Security and Privacy:
   - Strict security and privacy considerations must be applied at all stages, ensuring the protection of sensitive data and compliance with regulations.

- Continuous Monitoring:
   - A continuous monitoring system helps identify changes that may affect data quality, allowing for proactive adjustments.

- Education and Awareness:

- The team involved in geospatial data management must be educated on the importance of the data lifecycle to ensure good practices at all stages.

By understanding and properly following the geospatial data lifecycle, organizations and researchers can ensure their data remains relevant, reliable and useful over time, contributing to accurate analysis and informed decisions.

11.2. Data Collection and Update

Geospatial Data Collection and Update: Ensuring Accuracy and Relevance

The collection and updating of geospatial data are fundamental processes for maintaining the integrity and relevance of information about the geographic world. These processes involve different methods, from acquiring new data to maintaining existing information. Here is an explanation of these critical phases:

Geospatial Data Collection:

1. Remote Sensing:
   - *Description:* Use of satellites, drones or aircraft equipped with sensors to capture information about the Earth's surface. This approach is crucial for obtaining high-resolution images and land cover data.

2. Field Research:
   - *Description:* Physical displacement to specific locations to collect data directly. This may include topographic measurements, soil sampling, natural resource identification, and other data obtained on site.

3. Terrestrial Sensors:
   - *Description:* Sensors installed in strategic locations, such as weather stations or urban sensors, collect real-time data on specific conditions, such as temperature, humidity and air quality.

4. Crowdsourcing:
   - *Description:* Obtaining data from voluntary contributions from an online community. Applications and platforms allow users to send georeferenced information, such as photos or observations, enriching data sets.

Geospatial Data Update:

1. Continuous Monitoring:
   - *Description:* Use of real-time monitoring systems to capture dynamic changes in the environment. This includes urban changes, weather conditions and other variables that require frequent updates.

2. Periodic Satellite Images:

- *Description:* The acquisition of new satellite images at regular intervals to identify changes in land coverage, allowing for accurate map and model updates.

3. IoT Sensors (Internet of Things):
    - *Description:* The implementation of sensors connected to the internet, such as traffic sensors, environmental sensors and smart urban devices, which transmit data in real time, facilitating constant updating.

4. Integration with Dynamic Fonts:
    - *Description:* Establishment of automatic integrations with dynamic data sources, such as government databases, social media feeds or other online services that provide up-to-date information.

5. Community Feedback:
    - *Description:* Active community engagement in updating geospatial information. Users can report changes or corrections through interactive platforms.

Common Technologies:

1. GIS (Geographical Information Systems):
    - GIS tools are widely used for the manipulation, analysis and visualization of geospatial data, including updating processes.

2. Machine Learning and Artificial Intelligence:

- Machine learning algorithms can be used to analyze large sets of geospatial data and identify patterns, helping to automatically detect changes.

3. Remote Sensing Platforms:
- Specialized remote sensing platforms offer advanced capabilities for collecting and analyzing data from satellites, drones and other sources.

4. Mobile Applications:
- Mobile applications facilitate data collection in the field and enable instantaneous updating of georeferenced information.

The efficient collection and updating of geospatial data is essential to ensure that the information used in applications such as maps, urban analysis, and decision making reflects the reality of the geographic environment. With the evolution of technologies, the integration of traditional and innovative methods is essential to maintain accurate and updated data.

11.3. Data Quality and Consistency

Quality and Consistency of Geospatial Data: The Foundation for Accurate Decision Making

The quality and consistency of geospatial data plays a crucial role in the usefulness and reliability of that information. Ensuring that data is accurate, complete and consistent is essential for effective analysis, decision making and practical applications. Let's explore the main concepts related to these two essential characteristics of data:

Precision:

1. Definition:
   - Accuracy refers to the proximity between the information represented in geospatial data and the reality on the ground.

2. Maintenance and Update:
   - Accuracy is strongly influenced by data collection and updating processes. Information obtained through remote sensing, field surveys and other sources must be regularly reviewed and adjusted to reflect changes in the environment.

3. Technology Integration:
   - The incorporation of advanced technologies, such as high-precision global positioning systems (GPS) and high-resolution remote sensing, contributes to obtaining more accurate data from the initial collection phase.

4. Cross Validation:

- Verification through comparisons with reliable sources, such as official maps or reference data, is an important practice to validate the accuracy of geospatial data.

Integrity:

1. Definition:
- Data integrity involves ensuring that the information is complete, without omissions or corruptions.

2. Update Methods:
- Regular updates and effective gap-filling methods are crucial to maintaining the integrity of geospatial data. This includes incorporating new information and correcting outdated data.

3. Quality Control:
- The implementation of quality controls during the collection and updating processes is essential. This involves proactively detecting and correcting errors, inconsistencies and omissions.

Coherence:

1. Definition:

- Coherence refers to uniformity and consistency in geospatial data, ensuring that information is aligned internally and with other sources.

2. Data Standardization:
- The adoption of standards for data representation and storage contributes significantly to coherence. This includes the use of standardized coordinate systems, consistent units of measurement, and uniform nomenclature.

3. Synchronized Update:
- Ensuring that all geospatial data sources are updated in a synchronous manner is vital to avoid discrepancies and inconsistencies between different data sets.

Ensuring Quality and Consistency:

1. Continuous Monitoring:
- The implementation of continuous monitoring systems allows the rapid identification of quality problems and the application of immediate corrections.

2. Detailed Metadata:
- The inclusion of detailed metadata that describes the origin, collection method and any transformation applied to the data makes it easier to understand and evaluate its quality.

3. Training and Awareness:

- Training the team involved in managing geospatial data is crucial. A clear understanding of maintenance practices and the importance of quality contributes to data consistency.

The quality and consistency of geospatial data are fundamental foundations for effective analysis and decision-making. Implementing robust maintenance, updating, and quality control practices is essential to ensure that this data remains a reliable source of information about the geographic world.

11.4. Maintenance Tools

Geospatial Data Maintenance Tools: Ensuring Integrity and Accuracy

Efficiently maintaining geospatial data involves using specialized tools for updating, quality controlling, and correcting errors in datasets. Various software and technologies have been developed to optimize these processes, ensuring the integrity and accuracy of geographic information. Below, some common tools used in maintaining geospatial data are highlighted:

1. GIS (Geographical Information Systems):

- Description: GIS tools, such as ArcGIS, QGIS and GRASS GIS, are essential in maintaining geospatial data. They offer advanced functionalities for editing, updating and quality control of data. Features such as topology, field validation and editing tools simplify the process.

2. FME (Feature Manipulation Engine):
- Description: Safe Software's FME is a powerful platform for transforming and integrating geospatial data. It allows for the automation of workflows, making it easier to update data and correct inconsistencies. Its ability to support multiple formats makes it valuable in integrating different data sets.

3. PostgreSQL with PostGIS extension:
- Description: PostgreSQL, a relational database management system, when combined with the PostGIS spatial extension, provides a robust environment for storing, managing and updating geospatial data. PostGIS provides advanced spatial functionality such as spatial indexing and geometry operations.

4. GDAL (Geospatial Data Abstraction Library):
- Description: GDAL is a library that provides a set of tools for reading and writing geospatial data in various formats. It can be used in conjunction with other tools for format conversion, data projection and raster and vector manipulation.

5. OpenStreetMap (OSM):
- Description: The OpenStreetMap community and its associated tools provide a collaborative platform for collecting and updating geospatial data. Collaborative editing through the iD and JOSM editor allows users to contribute to the continuous improvement of the global map.

6. GeoTools:
- Description: GeoTools is a Java library that provides tools for processing and manipulating geospatial data. It is used in several Java applications to perform spatial operations, such as format conversion, spatial analysis, and geometry editing.

7. Quantum Spatial's SiteRecon:
- Description: SiteRecon is a tool specialized in evaluating and updating geospatial data related to utilities, such as water and sewage networks. It offers advanced error detection and large-scale data optimization capabilities.

8. ERDAS IMAGINE:
- Description: ERDAS IMAGINE is a comprehensive solution for image and raster data processing. It is widely used in maintaining data related to remote sensing, allowing the updating of images and mosaics with advanced tools.

9. Esri Data Reviewer:

- Description: Esri Data Reviewer is an ArcGIS extension that provides specialized tools for quality control and review of geospatial data. It allows the definition of rules and automatic checks to ensure data quality.

These tools play essential roles in maintaining geospatial data, providing efficiency, accuracy and quality control. Choosing the appropriate tool will depend on the specific needs of the project and the types of geospatial data involved.

11.5. Good Update Practices

Geospatial Data Update Best Practices: Ensuring Ongoing Accuracy and Relevance

Effectively maintaining geospatial data is vital to ensuring the accuracy, consistency and ongoing relevance of information. Good updating practices are fundamental to face the challenges associated with the dynamics of the geographic environment. Below are some key strategies for ensuring geospatial data quality over time:

1. Establish Regular Update Processes:
   - Implement systematic and regular processes for updating geospatial data. This may include periodic

reviews, automatic updates from external sources, and the integration of new data as it becomes available.

two. Involve Relevant Stakeholders:
   - Involving stakeholders is crucial. Collaborate with local experts, communities, and other entities who can contribute region-specific information. This not only enriches the data but also fosters an environment of collaboration.

3. Use Updated Data Sources:
   - Make sure the data sources used are up to date. This includes official maps, remote sensing data, government information, and contributions from mapping communities.

4. Implement Quality Controls:
   - Develop and implement quality controls to verify data integrity and accuracy. This may include automatic checks, manual reviews, and cross-validations with trusted sources.

5. Adopt Quality and Metadata Standards:
   - Establish and follow specific quality standards for geospatial data. This includes using detailed metadata that describes the origin, quality, and last update date of the data.

6. Make Use of Monitoring Technologies:
   - Implement continuous monitoring technologies to quickly identify changes, errors or inconsistencies in data. This allows for proactive fixes before issues negatively impact data quality.

7. Facilitate Collaborative Updates:
   - Promote a collaborative approach to updating data, especially on collaborative mapping platforms. Allow users to contribute local information, report changes, and participate in data validation.

8. Conduct Training and Awareness:
   - Provide regular training to the team responsible for data management. Make sure they are aware of best practices for updating, the latest technologies, and changes to relevant policies or standards.

9. Plan for Changes in the Environment:
   - Anticipate and plan for changes in the geographic environment. This could include extreme weather events, changes to urban infrastructure, or any other change that affects data accuracy.

10. Keep an Update History:
   - Keep a historical record of all updates made to geospatial data. This is crucial for tracking changes, assessing quality over time, and meeting audit requirements.

By incorporating these best practices, organizations can ensure their geospatial data is reliable, accurate and continually relevant, meeting the needs of users and applications in a dynamic environment.

Chapter 12: Trends and Future of Geospatial Databases

12.1. Emerging Technologies

Emerging Technologies in Geospatial Databases: Innovations and Impacts

The field of geospatial databases is constantly evolving, driven by technological advances that expand the capabilities of collecting, storing and analyzing geographic data. Some of the emerging technologies that are significantly shaping the field include:

1. Blockchain for Authenticity and Traceability:
    - Description: Blockchain technology, known for its security and immutability, is being explored to ensure the authenticity and traceability of geospatial data. This is particularly relevant in sectors such as supply chains and asset management, where data reliability is crucial.

two. Internet of Things (IoT) for Real-Time Capture:
    - Description: IoT device integration provides a real-time source of geospatial data. Sensors in vehicles, buildings and even personal devices generate data that can be integrated into geospatial databases, providing a dynamic and up-to-date view of the environment.

3. Machine Learning and Artificial Intelligence:

- Description: Machine learning (ML) and artificial intelligence (AI) techniques are being applied to analyzing geospatial data to extract complex patterns and valuable insights. This improves the ability to predict changes, detect anomalies, and optimize location-based processes.

4. Cloud Computing for Scalability:
   - Description: Cloud computing has revolutionized the ability to store and process geospatial data. Platforms such as AWS, Azure and Google Cloud offer services specific to spatial data, enabling scalability on demand and facilitating global collaboration.

5. Augmented Reality (AR) and Virtual Reality (VR):
   - Description: AR and VR are being used to visualize geospatial data in a more immersive way. This is especially valuable in urban planning, infrastructure design and training, providing a more intuitive understanding of the environment based on geospatial data.

6. Edge Computing for Real-Time Processing:
   - Description: Edge Computing takes data processing closer to the generation source, reducing latency. This is particularly beneficial for applications that require real-time responses, such as vehicle navigation and environmental monitoring.

7. Drones and Autonomous Vehicles:

- Description: Collecting geospatial data through drones and autonomous vehicles is becoming increasingly common. These technologies offer the ability to map large areas quickly and accurately, being applicable in sectors such as agriculture, environmental monitoring and infrastructure.

8. 3D Geographic Information Systems (GIS):
- Description: The evolution of GIS to include three-dimensional representations is allowing a more complete understanding of the environment. This is vital in sectors such as architecture, engineering and urban planning, where height and topography are critical factors.

These emerging technologies not only expand the capabilities of geospatial databases, but also transform the way we interact with and take advantage of geographic information. As these innovations continue to develop, they are expected to provide more efficient solutions and deeper insights for a variety of applications.

12.2. Artificial Intelligence and Machine Learning

Artificial Intelligence (AI) and Machine Learning (ML) in Geospatial Databases: Transforming Data into Insights

The integration of artificial intelligence and machine learning into geospatial databases represents a revolution in the way we interpret and use geographic data. These technologies enable systems to learn complex patterns, perform predictive analytics, and optimize location-related processes. Below, we highlight how AI and ML are positively influencing geospatial databases:

1. Predictive Analysis:
   - Description: AI and ML systems are capable of analyzing large sets of geospatial data to identify patterns and trends. This allows you to create predictive models to predict future events, such as weather patterns, traffic movements, or environmental changes.

Practical Example: A predictive analytics system using geospatial data can predict traffic congestion patterns in urban areas based on past events, weather conditions and special events.

two. Anomaly Detection:
   - Description: ML algorithms can be trained to identify anomalies in geospatial data. This is valuable for detecting unusual behavior, such as suspicious activity in certain regions, sudden environmental changes, or critical infrastructure failures.

Practical Example: An anomaly detection system can identify atypical vehicle movement patterns in an area, indicating possible unusual activities.

3. Route and Navigation Optimization:
   - Description: ML algorithms can analyze geospatial data in real time to optimize navigation routes. This leads to more efficient navigation, considering variables such as traffic, weather conditions and specific events.

Practical Example: A navigation application that uses machine learning can suggest alternative routes in real time based on information about congestion and recent accidents.

4. Image Classification and Pattern Recognition:
   - Description: Computer vision techniques, a subarea of AI, are used to classify and recognize patterns in geospatial images. This is valuable for identifying geographic features such as land cover types or landscape changes.

Practical Example: Using satellite images, an AI system can automatically classify urban areas, forests and bodies of water, providing detailed information about land use.

5. Personalizing Location-Based Recommendations:
   - Description: AI-powered recommendation systems can offer personalized suggestions based on the user's location. This is applicable in sectors such as commerce, tourism and entertainment.

Practical Example: A recommendation application can suggest restaurants, stores or cultural events based on the user's historical preferences and current location.

Applying artificial intelligence and machine learning to geospatial databases not only provides operational efficiencies, but also opens up new possibilities for understanding and interacting with the world around us. These technologies are driving the evolution of geographic information systems, enabling more advanced analyzes and more accurate insights.

12.3. Augmented Reality and Virtual Reality

Integration of Augmented and Virtual Reality in Geospatial Databases: A Futuristic Vision

The integration of augmented reality (AR) and virtual reality (VR) with geospatial databases is marking a significant advancement in the way we interact with and visualize geographic data. These technologies not only improve the presentation of information, but also provide more immersive and interactive experiences. Let's explore how AR and VR intertwine with geospatial databases:

1. Augmented Reality:
   - Description: AR combines virtual elements with the real environment, providing an overlay of geospatial information on the real world. Devices such as

smartphones and AR glasses enable users to view contextualized data in real time while interacting with the surrounding environment.

How This Improves the Geospatial Experience:
- AR allows geographic data, such as information about points of interest or map layers, to be overlaid in real time on the physical environment. For example, by pointing a smartphone at a building, information about its history or current use can be displayed.

two. Virtual reality:
- Description: VR creates completely virtual environments, immersive and independent of the real world. Using devices such as VR glasses, users are transported to simulated environments, providing a visual and interactive experience rich in details.

How This Improves the Geospatial Experience:
- Virtual environments created by VR can represent geographic areas in a detailed and three-dimensional way. This is valuable for urban simulations, infrastructure planning and training in specific geographic contexts.

3. Practical Applications:
- Exploration of the Environment:
- Using AR, users can explore geographic areas with real-time contextual information, such as historical details or reviews of local services.

- Urban planning:
- VR can be used to create interactive simulations of urban projects, allowing stakeholders to visualize and evaluate proposals in a more realistic way.

- Geographic Education:
- Both technologies are valuable for geography education, providing students with hands-on and visual experiences to understand complex geography concepts.

4. Challenges and Opportunities:
- Challenges:
- Issues related to accuracy when overlaying information in AR.
- Need for specialized hardware for immersive VR experiences.

- Opportunities:
- Improved understanding and interpretation of geospatial data.
- Innovative applications in sectors such as tourism, education and urban planning.

The integration of AR and VR with geospatial databases represents a new frontier in visualizing and interacting with geographic data. These technologies have the potential to transform the way we perceive and use spatial information, offering more immersive experiences aligned with the demands of an increasingly digital and interconnected world.

12.4. Predictive Analytics

Predictive Analytics in Geospatial Databases: Anticipating Trends for Informed Decision Making

Predictive analytics, an advanced form of data analysis, is increasingly being incorporated into geospatial databases, providing deeper, more proactive insight into geographic behavior. This approach uses prediction algorithms to anticipate patterns and trends in spatial data, offering valuable information for various applications. Let's explore how predictive analytics is transforming geospatial data management:

1. Spatial Pattern Modeling:
  - Description: Machine learning algorithms are trained with historical geospatial data to identify spatial patterns and relationships. These models are then used to predict future behaviors based on new data.

Practical example:
  - Predictive models can identify patterns of population movement in urban areas, allowing to anticipate

demands for public services, transport and urban planning.

two. Forecast of Climate Events and Natural Disasters:
   - Description: Algorithms analyze meteorological, geographic and historical data to predict extreme weather events, such as storms or floods, allowing preventive actions.

Practical example:
   - Predictive analysis can anticipate areas prone to landslides based on topographic data, historical rainfall and soil conditions.

3. Route and Traffic Optimization:
   - Description: Algorithms predict traffic patterns based on historical and real-time data, optimizing routes to reduce congestion and improve transport efficiency.

Practical example:
   - Predictive navigation systems can suggest alternative routes based on current conditions and traffic forecasts.

4. Urban Planning and Demand for Space:
   - Description: Predictive models assist in urban planning by predicting the demand for space in different areas of the city, considering factors such as population growth and economic development.

Practical example:

- Population growth forecasts are used to plan the expansion of urban infrastructure, such as schools, parks and transport networks.

5. Identifying Trends in Business Data:

- Description: Companies use predictive analysis on geospatial data to identify market trends, optimize supply chains and make strategic decisions.

Practical example:

- Retailers can predict product demand in different regions based on historical sales data and demographic characteristics.

Predictive analytics in geospatial databases not only provides a more holistic view of the geographic environment, but also empowers decision makers to act proactively. By anticipating trends and events, organizations can prepare more effectively, mitigate risks and respond quickly to changes in the geospatial landscape, resulting in more informed and efficient decisions.

12.5. Future Challenges

Future Challenges in Geospatial Databases: Navigating the Horizons of Complexity

As we move toward a future driven by technological innovation, geospatial databases will face significant challenges that demand smart, adaptable solutions. Let's explore some of these emerging challenges that will shape the geospatial database landscape in the coming years:

1. Large Data Management:
   - Challenge: The exponential growth in the generation of geospatial data, coming from remote sensors, mobile devices and other sources, represents a challenge to the ability to store, process and efficiently retrieve this data.

   - Potential Solution: Continuous development of distributed storage techniques, large-scale processing and data compression algorithms to handle large volumes without compromising efficiency.

two. Interoperability between Different Systems:
   - Challenge: The diversity of geospatial database systems and data standards makes interoperability difficult, hindering the ability to efficiently share information between different platforms.

   - Potential Solution: Adoption of open standards and interoperable protocols, in addition to the development of interfaces that allow frictionless communication between different systems.

3. Ethical Considerations and Privacy:
   - Challenge: The intensive use of geospatial data raises ethical concerns related to privacy, security and potential excessive monitoring of individuals.

   - Potential Solution: Strict implementation of privacy policies, anonymization of sensitive data and transparency in the collection and use of geospatial information.

4. Adaptation to Emerging Technologies:
   - Challenge: The rapid evolution of technologies such as artificial intelligence, augmented reality and virtual reality requires geospatial databases to adapt to support these innovations.

   - Potential Solution: Continuous investment in research and development to efficiently integrate new technologies into existing systems, ensuring their compatibility and synergy.

5. Climate Change and Geospatial Resilience:
   - Challenge: The increase in climate change requires a geospatial approach to understand and mitigate impacts. The resilience of geospatial data in the face of these changes is crucial.

   - Potential Solution: Development of advanced predictive models to assess and anticipate climate impacts, as well as investment in backup and redundancy strategies to ensure data resilience.

Addressing these challenges will require close collaboration between academic communities, the private sector and governments. Continuous innovation, combined with an ethical and user-centric approach, will be key to ensuring that geospatial databases continue to play a vital role in understanding and managing our changing world.

Chapter 13: Case Studies 1

13.1. Case 1: Implementation of a Geospatial Data Management System in a City Hall

Case Study: Implementation of a Geospatial Data Management System in a City Hall

1. Context:
A medium-sized city hall, facing increasing challenges in terms of urbanization, infrastructure management and provision of public services, decided to adopt a Geospatial Data Management System (SGDG) to optimize its operations. The city experienced rapid population growth and, consequently, an increased demand for efficient public services. The need to make informed decisions, especially in urban planning, waste management, and urban mobility projects, has been identified as a priority.

2. Goals:
The main objectives of this project were:
- Data Centralization: Consolidate geospatial data dispersed across different municipal departments into a centralized system, eliminating information silos.
- Improvement in Decision Making: Empower city hall with tools that enable spatial analysis for more informed decision-making on urban issues.
- Operational Efficiency: Increase operational efficiency in areas such as waste management, urban planning and infrastructure maintenance.

- Improved Public Services: Improve the delivery of public services, including optimizing routes for waste collection, public transport planning and emergency response.

3. Implementation:
The implementation of the SGDG was carried out in several stages:
- Needs Assessment: Carry out a detailed analysis of the specific needs of each department, identifying the geospatial data sets relevant to their operations.
- Infrastructure Development: Implement the SGDG infrastructure, including choosing and configuring a spatial database, defining data standards and integrating with existing systems.
- Data Acquisition: Collect geospatial data from various sources, such as urban sensors, topographic surveys and information from public services.
- Integration with Existing Systems: Ensure smooth integration of the SGDG with the city hall's existing information systems to avoid operational interruptions.
- Training and Capacity Building: Provide training for municipal employees on the use of SGDG, ensuring that the team is able to effectively explore the system's functionalities.

4. Expected Benefits:
- Informed Decision Making: SGDG enabled city hall to make more informed decisions by providing a comprehensive spatial view of urban operations.

- Improved Operational Efficiency: Optimizing routes for services such as waste collection has led to a reduction in operational costs and more efficient use of municipal resources.
- Infrastructure Management: The ability to monitor and manage urban infrastructure, such as roads and water networks, has been improved, allowing the implementation of proactive maintenance actions.
- Improved Public Services: The population experienced tangible improvements in the quality of public services, such as more efficient waste collection and better traffic management.

This case study highlights how the implementation of an SGDG can be a catalyst for positive transformation in a city hall, enabling it to face urban challenges in a more effective, efficient and sustainable way.

13.2. Challenges and Solutions

Challenges and Solutions in the Implementation of the Geospatial Data Management System at City Hall

The implementation of a Geospatial Data Management System (SGDG) in a city hall presents specific challenges that require careful approaches and innovative solutions. During the implementation process in the city hall in question, some crucial challenges were identified, and specific strategies were adopted to overcome them:

1. Diversity of Data Sources:
Challenge: Integrating data from different sources, such as urban sensors, topographic surveys and existing city hall systems, proved to be complex due to the heterogeneity of these sources.
Solution: Implementation of robust data integration tools that could handle different formats and standards. Adoption of normalization protocols to ensure data consistency.

two. Resistance to change:
Challenge: The introduction of an SGDG represented a significant change in traditional work practices, meeting resistance from some employees.
Solution: Development of personalized training programs for different departments, emphasizing the practical benefits of SGDG. Inclusion of the team from the early phases of the project also helped alleviate resistance.

3. Integration with Existing Systems:
Challenge: Ensure smooth integration with city hall's existing information systems, avoiding operational interruptions.
Solution: Development of personalized integration interfaces, using recognized interoperability standards. Implementation was carried out in phases, allowing for continuous testing and adjustments as needed.

4. Continuous Data Collection and Update:
Challenge: Keep geospatial data updated in a dynamic environment, where urban changes and unforeseen events are frequent.
Solution: Implementation of an automated real-time data collection system, integrating sensors and dynamic sources. Establishing regular update protocols to ensure continued accuracy.

5. Data Security Guarantee:
Challenge: Protect sensitive geospatial data against cyber threats and ensure compliance with privacy regulations.
Solution: Implementation of advanced cybersecurity protocols, including robust encryption and granular access control. Regular audits were conducted to ensure compliance with security standards.

6. Adaptation to Urban Changes:
Challenge: The rapid evolution of the urban landscape required constant adaptation of the SGDG to reflect changes.
Solution: Implementation of a flexible system that could be easily updated to incorporate changes in urban infrastructure. Continuous monitoring of the urban landscape using sensors and regular database updates.

These challenges and solutions during the implementation of SGDG at City Hall highlight the importance of a flexible approach, proactive stakeholder engagement, and the application of advanced technologies to ensure the continued success of the system. Continuous learning and adaptation are key in a dynamic urban environment.

13.3. Results Obtained

Results Obtained with the Implementation of the Geospatial Data Management System

The successful implementation of the Geospatial Data Management System (SGDG) at the city hall has resulted in a series of tangible benefits, fundamentally transforming the way the administration handles geospatial data. The results obtained include:

1. Improvement in Operational Efficiency:
Before the implementation of the SGDG, processes related to geospatial data management were often time-consuming and prone to errors due to the diversity of sources and systems. With the introduction of SGDG, there was a notable improvement in operational efficiency. The automation of routine tasks, data standardization and smooth integration between different systems have provided significant gains in terms of time and resources.

two. More Informed Decision Making:

Easy and fast access to accurate geospatial data became a reality after the implementation of SGDG. Decision makers now have up-to-date information and clear views of the urban landscape, enabling a more in-depth and informed analysis. This has resulted in more informed decisions in a range of areas, from urban planning to emergency management.

3. Resource Optimization and Strategic Planning:

The ability to visualize and analyze geospatial data in real time allowed the city to optimize resources more efficiently. For example, in planning waste collection routes, optimization based on geospatial data has led to a reduction in operational costs and time spent. Furthermore, the SGDG facilitated the development of long-term strategies for sustainable urban growth.

4. More Effective Response to Emergency Situations:

The ability to quickly map areas affected by events such as floods, fires or other natural disasters has proven crucial. The SGDG enabled a more effective response to emergency situations, facilitating coordinated evacuation, allocation of relief resources and damage mitigation.

5. Enhanced Collaboration between Departments:

The integration of SGDG with different city hall departments promoted closer collaboration and a shared understanding of geospatial data. This reduced information silos and promoted a more holistic approach to planning and executing urban projects.

6. Long-Term Cost Reduction:
Although the initial investment in implementing the SGDG is significant, the results obtained show a substantial reduction in costs in the long term. Operational efficiency, resource optimization and informed decision-making have contributed to considerable savings in various aspects of urban administration.

These results demonstrate the positive impact that a Geospatial Data Management System can have on public administration, highlighting its crucial role in the digital transformation of cities for more efficient and sustainable management.

13.4. Lessons Learned

Lessons Learned in Implementing the Geospatial Data Management System (SGDG)

The implementation of the SGDG provided a series of valuable lessons that covered both technical and organizational aspects. These lessons offer

valuable   insights   to   guide   future   similar
implementations:

1. Stakeholder Involvement and Understanding:
        One of the critical factors for success was the
effective   involvement   and   understanding   of
stakeholders.   Including   representatives   from   all
departments involved from the initial phases allowed a
more in-depth understanding of the specific needs of
each sector, resulting in a solution more adapted to the
real demands of the city hall.

two. Data Standardization is Fundamental:
        Data standardization proved to be essential to
ensure   consistency   and   interoperability   between
different systems. Defining clear standards for the
collection, storage, and formatting of geospatial data
has simplified the integration of heterogeneous sources
and made it easier for multiple departments to use this
data.

3. Continuous Training Required:
        The   complexity   of   the   SGDG   required   a
significant   training   effort   for   employees.   The
implementation of ongoing training programs, which
covered   both   technical   aspects   and   operational
processes, was crucial to ensure that the team was
trained and comfortable with the new tool.

4. Adaptation to Organizational Changes:

The introduction of a SGDG often implies organizational changes. Resistance to change can be overcome through effective communication, employee involvement from the beginning, and continuous demonstration of the benefits the new solution brings to daily operations.

5. Data Security is a Priority:
Geospatial data security was a priority from the beginning. Implementing robust security policies, including access control, auditing and encryption, was essential to protect sensitive information and ensure compliance with privacy regulations.

6. Scalability is Important for the Future:
When designing SGDG, consideration of scalability was key. The system must be able to handle a substantial increase in data and demands as the city grows. Choosing technologies and architectures that can easily scale ensures that the system continues to meet future needs.

7. Continuous Monitoring and Feedback:
SGDG implementation did not end with the initial launch; it was a continuous process of monitoring and adjustments. Collecting constant feedback from users, monitoring system performance, and being ready to adjust as needed were essential practices to ensure continued effectiveness.

8. Strategic Partnerships with Suppliers:
Developing strategic partnerships with technology providers is crucial. Maintaining a constant dialogue with suppliers, ensuring regular updates and ongoing technical support, is vital to face unforeseen challenges and take advantage of technological innovations.

These lessons learned provide a solid foundation for future SGDG implementations, highlighting the importance of collaboration, flexibility and a user-oriented approach throughout the process.

13.5. Recommendations

Recommendations for Implementing Geospatial Data Management Systems (SGDG)

Based on the case study of the successful implementation of the SGDG in a city hall, the following recommendations are offered for organizations that are considering or planning to implement a Geospatial Data Management System:

1. Proactive Stakeholder Engagement:
Ensure the proactive participation of representatives from all sectors involved from the beginning of the process. The continuous involvement of stakeholders helps to understand the specific needs of

each department, ensuring a solution that is more aligned with the organization's real demands.

two. Development of Data Standards:
Establish clear standards for collecting, storing, and formatting geospatial data. This facilitates interoperability between different systems and simplifies the integration of heterogeneous sources, ensuring data consistency.

3. Investment in Continuous Training:
Recognize the importance of ongoing training for staff. Provide comprehensive training programs that address both the technical aspects and operational processes of the SGDG. This is essential to ensure that the team is capable and comfortable with the new tool.

4. Adaptation to Organizational Changes:
Anticipate and manage organizational changes that may be triggered by the implementation of the SGDG. Resistance to change can be mitigated through effective communication, employee engagement, and continuous demonstration of the tangible benefits of the new solution.

5. Emphasis on Data Security:
Prioritize geospatial data security from the start. Implement robust security policies, including access control, auditing, and encryption, to protect sensitive

information and ensure compliance with privacy regulations.

6. Planning for Scalability:
Consider scalability as a key element of planning. Choose technologies and architectures that can easily scale to handle a substantial increase in data and demands as your organization grows.

7. Continuous Monitoring and Feedback:
View SGDG implementation as an ongoing process. Collect constant feedback from users, monitor system performance, and be ready to adjust as needed. Continuous adaptation is essential to ensure effectiveness over time.

8. Establishment of Strategic Partnerships:
Develop strategic partnerships with technology providers. Maintaining a constant dialogue with suppliers, ensuring regular updates and continuous technical support are essential to face unforeseen challenges and take advantage of technological innovations.

By following these recommendations, organizations will be better prepared to implement SGDG effectively, making the most of the benefits that efficient geospatial data management can offer.

Chapter 14: Case Studies 2

14.1. Case 2: Application of Geospatial Data in Precision Agriculture

Case Study: Application of Geospatial Data in Precision Agriculture

The application of geospatial data in precision agriculture is exemplified by an innovative project implemented on a large-scale farm. The farm, specialized in grain cultivation, faced challenges related to optimizing the use of resources, increasing operational efficiency and reducing environmental impact. Faced with these challenges, the farm decided to adopt a geospatial data-driven approach to improve its agricultural practices.

The main objectives of the project were:

1. Optimization of Input Use: Use geospatial data to map variability in the soil, allowing personalized application of fertilizers, pesticides and irrigation.

2. Crop Growth Monitoring: Implement continuous monitoring systems using sensors and satellite images to assess crop growth and identify areas that require specific intervention.

3. Reducing Waste of Resources: Minimize the waste of resources, such as water and inputs, through precise

and targeted application, resulting in economic and environmental benefits.

4. Increased Productivity: Utilize geospatial data to make informed decisions that would lead to an overall increase in farm productivity.

Geospatial Technology Integration:
Geospatial technology has been integrated in several crucial ways:

1. Remote Sensing: Using satellite and drone images to obtain data on plant health, land cover and terrain variability.

2. Field Data Collection: Use of geospatial data collection devices in the field, such as GNSS receivers on agricultural machinery, to record real-time information about soil variability.

3. Geographical Information Systems (GIS): Implementation of GIS for spatial data analysis, allowing the creation of maps of soil variability, crop growth patterns and intervention zones.

4. Data Processing Algorithms: Development and implementation of data processing algorithms to transform raw data into actionable information, such as input application maps.

Results Obtained:

The application of geospatial data in precision agriculture has resulted in several significant benefits:

1. Resource Use Efficiency: The personalized application of inputs has led to a substantial reduction in the use of fertilizers and pesticides, resulting in financial savings and lower environmental impact.

2. Increased Productivity: Continuous monitoring allowed real-time adjustments, resulting in an improvement in crop productivity.

3. Informed Decision Making: Farmers began to make more informed decisions, based on accurate data about the condition of the soil and crops.

4. Environmental Sustainability: The reduction in the use of inputs and targeted practice contributed to more sustainable agricultural practices.

Lessons Learned:
During the course of the project, some valuable lessons were learned:

1. Training Needs: The agricultural team required significant training to understand and make the most of geospatial tools.

2. Data Integration: Effective integration of different data sources such as satellite data and data collected in the field was crucial to obtain a holistic view.

3. Continuous Maintenance and Updating: Geospatial technology requires ongoing maintenance and updating to ensure ongoing accuracy and relevance.

Based on this case study, future implementations of precision agriculture with geospatial data can benefit from incorporating:

1. Emerging Technologies: Explore new technologies, such as artificial intelligence, for advanced geospatial data analysis.

2. Collaboration with Experts: Partnerships with geospatial experts can further improve the effectiveness of data application in agriculture.

3. Scalability: Plan for scalability, especially on farms that plan to expand their operations.

The application of geospatial data in precision agriculture is a compelling example of how technology can transform traditional sectors, bringing efficiency, sustainability and informed decision-making.

14.2. Project description

Project Description: Application of Geospatial Data in Precision Agriculture

The project in question was developed on a medium-sized farm that sought to optimize its agricultural practices through the application of geospatial data. The farm faced challenges related to soil variability, efficiency in the use of inputs and wanted to increase the productivity of its crops. Faced with these challenges, the decision was made to implement a precision agriculture system based on geospatial information.

Data collect:

Data collection was a crucial phase of the project. Different sources were used, including:

1. Satellite and Drone Imagery: To get a detailed look at the topography, plant health and other physical characteristics of the field.

2. Sensors in the Field: Geospatial data collection devices, such as GNSS receivers on agricultural machinery, have been used to record real-time information during field operations.

3. Historical Farm Data: Historical farm information such as records of previous harvests and growth patterns have been integrated for comparative analysis.

Tools Used:

The project used a variety of specialized tools to handle geospatial data:

1. Geographical Information Systems (GIS): GIS tools were employed to analyze and visualize spatial data, creating detailed maps of soil variability.

2. Image Processing Algorithms: Algorithms have been developed to process satellite and drone images, extract relevant information about plant health, and identify areas of interest.

3. Remote Sensing Platforms: Platforms that allowed the easy integration of data from different sources, facilitating a more comprehensive analysis.

Application of Geospatial Information:
Geospatial information has been applied in several areas of precision agriculture:

1. Soil Variability Mapping: Using data from sensors and satellite images, the farm was able to map soil variability, identifying areas with different characteristics.

2. Personalized Application of Inputs: Based on soil variability maps, personalized application of inputs, such as fertilizers and irrigation, was implemented, optimizing the use of these resources.

3. Crop Growth Monitoring: Continuous monitoring using sensors made it possible to identify crop growth patterns, enabling specific interventions when necessary.

The project results were significant, with tangible benefits, such as:

1. Cost Reduction: The personalized application of inputs resulted in a substantial reduction in operating costs.

2. Increased Productivity: Continuous monitoring and targeted application contributed to an increase in crop productivity.

3. Sustainability: Optimizing the use of resources had positive impacts on the environmental sustainability of the farm.

Lessons Learned and Recommendations:
The project highlighted the importance of efficient integration of geospatial data and the need for training for the team involved. Recommendations include continually updating data, exploring emerging

technologies, and collaborating with geospatial experts to further improve results.

14.3. Benefits of Geospatial Technology

Benefits of Geospatial Technology in the Precision Agriculture Project:

The application of geospatial technology in this specific precision agriculture project provided a series of substantial benefits, positively impacting processes and results. These benefits cover several areas, from optimizing the use of inputs to increasing operational efficiency and improving the quality of agricultural products.

1. Accuracy in the Application of Inputs:
The use of geospatial data allowed the creation of detailed maps of soil variability, identifying areas with distinct characteristics. This precision in understanding soil variability has resulted in personalized application of inputs such as fertilizers and irrigation. The targeted distribution of these inputs according to the specific needs of each area contributed to more efficient use, reducing costs and minimizing waste.

two. Resource Usage Optimization:
Continuous collection of geospatial data, including information on crop growth and soil variability,

has made it possible to optimize resource use. This included effective irrigation management, ensuring water was applied only where needed, and dynamically adapting fertilizer application according to specific soil conditions in different parts of the field. The resulting optimization has led to a significant reduction in resource waste, promoting sustainability and environmental responsibility.

3. Increased Productivity and Quality of Agricultural Products:

Precise application of inputs, combined with continuous monitoring of crop growth, has contributed to a substantial increase in agricultural productivity. Furthermore, the quality of agricultural products was improved, since interventions were carried out in a specific and personalized way. This resulted in healthier and more consistent harvests, meeting higher quality standards.

4. Informed Decision Making:

The ability to analyze geospatial data in real time gave the farm team a solid foundation for making informed decisions. Analyzing soil variability maps, satellite images and sensor data has allowed farmers to identify patterns, anticipate potential problems and adjust their strategies as needed.

5. Improved Operational Efficiency:

The implementation of geospatial technology has resulted in an overall improvement in the farm's operational efficiency. Agricultural processes were optimized, from soil preparation to harvest, with the application of inputs and resource management being conducted in a more intelligent and targeted manner.

Geospatial technology has played a key role in transforming agricultural practices, providing significant benefits in terms of operational efficiency, resource optimization and quality of agricultural products. These benefits have not only positively impacted the farm's economic results, but have also contributed to a more sustainable and responsible approach to farm management.

14.4. Impact on Agriculture

Direct Impact of Geospatial Technology on Agriculture:

The introduction and application of geospatial technology in agriculture has had a profound and positive impact on various aspects of agricultural practice. This technological revolution has brought significant benefits ranging from more accurate decision-making to efficient optimization of resources and an overall improvement in agricultural production performance.

1. Precise Decision Making:

Geospatial technology provides farmers with a detailed, real-time view of field conditions. Analyzing geospatial data, such as soil variability maps, satellite imagery, and location-specific climate data, empowers farmers to make more accurate decisions. This includes selecting suitable crops for specific areas of the field, accurately scheduling irrigation, and personalized application of agricultural inputs. Informed decision-making contributes significantly to the success of the harvest.

two. Efficient Resource Management:
With geospatial data, farmers can manage their resources more efficiently. Irrigation can be adjusted according to the specific needs of each area of the field, minimizing water waste. The application of fertilizers and pesticides can be adapted based on soil characteristics, resulting in more efficient use of these inputs. Efficient resource management not only reduces costs but also promotes sustainable agricultural practices.

3. Planting and Harvest Optimization:
Geospatial data is crucial for optimizing planting and harvesting. Farmers can plan crop distribution according to the specific conditions of each part of the field, taking into account factors such as soil quality and sun exposure. This not only increases harvesting efficiency, but also contributes to a more even and effective distribution of crops.

4. Crop Growth Monitoring:

Geospatial technology allows for continuous monitoring of crop growth. Satellite and drone imagery can capture detailed visual data, while sensors in the field provide real-time information about the state of plants. This precise monitoring enables early detection of problems, such as pests or diseases, allowing for quick and effective corrective actions.

5. Accuracy in Forecasting Risks and Climate Variabilities:

Geospatial data analysis also contributes to a better understanding and prediction of climate risks and variability. This allows farmers to prepare for extreme weather events, adjust their farming practices as needed, and minimize adverse impacts on crops.

The direct impact of geospatial technology on agriculture is substantial. By empowering farmers with detailed information about the growing environment, this technology is redefining the way decisions are made, resources are managed and agricultural production is optimized, contributing to more sustainable and efficient agriculture.

14.5. Next steps

Next Steps in the Application of Geospatial Data in Precision Agriculture:

The project to apply geospatial data in precision agriculture clearly demonstrated the benefits and opportunities provided by this innovative approach. To advance further and maximize results, the next steps should focus on optimizations, expansions and strategic integrations. Here are some considerations for the next steps of the project:

1. Integration of New Data Sources:
Exploring and integrating new sources of geospatial data can further enrich agricultural analysis and decisions. This may include the use of advanced sensors, more detailed weather data, high-resolution satellite imagery, and region-specific weather information. Diversifying data sources can provide a more comprehensive understanding of field conditions.

two. Implementation of Emerging Technologies:
Considering the implementation of emerging technologies such as artificial intelligence (AI) and machine learning (ML) can lead to more advanced and predictive analytics. ML algorithms can be trained to recognize complex patterns in geospatial data, offering valuable insights for agricultural decision-making.

3. Development of User-Friendly Interfaces:
Investing in developing more intuitive and accessible user interfaces can facilitate farmers'

continued adoption of the technology. This includes creating easy-to-use dashboards, user-friendly mobile apps, and custom reports that enable users to access and interpret geospatial data effectively.

4. Remote Monitoring and Automation:

Exploring remote monitoring and automation solutions can increase operational efficiency. The use of drones for regular field monitoring, automated irrigation systems based on geospatial data and the implementation of autonomous agricultural practices are areas that can be explored to further optimize processes.

5. Collaboration and Data Sharing:

Promoting collaboration and data sharing between farmers, researchers and stakeholders can create a robust information network. This can result in broader collective insights, shared better agricultural practices, and a more resilient community.

6. Environmental Impact Assessment:

Consider the implementation of tools that allow the assessment of the environmental impact of agricultural practices. This may involve analyzing the sustainable use of water, minimizing the use of chemicals and promoting biodiversity in growing areas.

7. Continuing Education and Training:

Investing in ongoing educational programs and training for end users is crucial. This will ensure that farmers are up to date on the latest technologies and can maximize the benefits of geospatial data in their daily operations.

By taking a strategic approach to project evolution, considering the integration of new technologies, expanding the data source and focusing on usability, it is possible to ensure that the application of geospatial data in precision agriculture continues to evolve in a meaningful way, providing lasting benefits for farmers and the sector as a whole.

Chapter 15: Case Studies 3

15.1. Case 3: Use of Geospatial Data in Natural Resource Management

Project Description: Use of Geospatial Data in Natural Resource Management

The project to use geospatial data in natural resource management was initiated in response to the growing need for sustainable approaches in managing ecosystems and preserving biodiversity. The context involved a geographic region rich in natural resources, but also subject to environmental challenges and climate change.

The project's main objectives included implementing effective natural resource management practices, monitoring ecosystems, assessing environmental impacts, and promoting data-driven decisions for long-term sustainability. The use of geospatial data was crucial to achieving these objectives, providing a detailed understanding of the geographic distribution of natural resources, ecosystems and environmental threats.

Geospatial Data Application:
1. Ecosystem Mapping: Using geospatial data from satellites and remote sensing, it was possible to accurately map the different ecosystems in the region, including forests, wetlands, and coastal zones. This

allowed a detailed understanding of the distribution of biodiversity.

2. Climate Change Monitoring: Geospatial data was employed to monitor climate change, including variations in snow cover, rainfall patterns, and temperature. This information was crucial for assessing the impacts of climate change on local ecosystems.

3. Water Resources Management: The use of geospatial data has facilitated the efficient management of water resources. This included monitoring water levels in rivers and lakes, identifying drought-prone areas, and optimizing water use for agricultural activities.

4. Environmental Risk Assessment: Geospatial analysis was applied to identify areas of environmental risk, such as landslides, floods and forest fires. This allowed the implementation of preventative strategies and rapid response to extreme weather events.

5. Conservation Planning: Geospatial data were fundamental in the development of conservation plans, identifying priority areas for protecting biodiversity, creating natural reserves and promoting sustainable land use practices.

The project results were significant. The application of geospatial data provided a holistic view of the region's natural resources, enabling more informed and efficient management. Benefits included:

- Informed Decision Making: Authorities and managers were empowered to make informed decisions based on accurate, real-time geospatial data.

- Environmental Sustainability: Data-driven management practices contributed to the promotion of environmental sustainability, ensuring the preservation of vital ecosystems.

- Emergency Response: Continuous monitoring allowed rapid response to extreme weather events and natural disasters, minimizing damage and protecting local communities.

- Efficiency in Resource Allocation: The allocation of resources for conservation and ecosystem management was optimized based on the needs identified by geospatial data.

Lessons Learned:
The project highlighted the importance of an integrated approach, involving multiple stakeholders, including local communities, scientists, and government authorities. Furthermore, he emphasized the need to invest in capacity building to ensure that stakeholders can fully leverage the benefits of geospatial data.

Next steps:

Next steps include expanding the project to cover additional areas, incorporating emerging technologies

15.2. Project Context

Project Context: Natural Resource Management with Geospatial Data

The natural resource management project was designed in response to the critical need to preserve and manage natural resources in a specific geographic region. The focus area covers a diverse range, including terrestrial ecosystems, aquatic areas and coastal zones. This region, rich in biodiversity and natural resources, faces environmental challenges that require a careful approach to ensure long-term sustainability.

Geographical Area Covered:
The project focuses on a specific geographic area, encompassing vast tracts of land, bodies of water, and coastal ecosystems. The delimitation of the area takes into account not only political borders, but also the natural characteristics and the interconnection of ecosystems present in the region.

Types of Managed Natural Resources:
Managed natural resources encompass a variety of elements, including forests, wetlands, water bodies,

biodiversity and coastal areas. Each of these resources plays a crucial role in maintaining ecological balance, sustaining wildlife, providing ecosystem services and, in many cases, sustaining local human communities.

Geospatial Data Integration:

Geospatial data integration is the backbone of the project. Using advanced remote sensing technologies, global positioning systems (GPS) and geospatial modeling, the project mapped the distribution of natural resources in the area in detail. Satellite images were used to monitor changes in vegetation cover, identify climate patterns and evaluate topography dynamics.

Furthermore, the use of geospatial data allowed the development of detailed ecosystem maps, identifying areas of significant biodiversity and places vulnerable to environmental threats. These data are crucial for formulating management strategies aimed at conservation, sustainable use and restoration of ecosystems.

Geospatial modeling has also played a vital role in risk analysis, assessing areas prone to adverse natural events such as floods, wildfires and coastal erosion. This provided a solid foundation for developing emergency mitigation and response strategies.

Geospatial data integration not only provides an in-depth understanding of the region's geography, but also empowers decision makers, environmental managers and local communities with accurate information to guide sustainable management of natural resources.

15.3. Environmental Results

Environmental Results: Contributions of Management Based on Geospatial Data

Implementing a geospatial data-based management approach has revealed a number of significant environmental outcomes, providing tangible benefits for the preservation, monitoring and enhancement of natural resources in the region.

1. Biodiversity Preservation:
Detailed analysis of biodiversity through geospatial data allowed the identification of critical areas for the preservation of local fauna and flora. This information guided the creation of conservation areas, contributing to the maintenance of ecosystems and the protection of threatened species.

two. Ecosystem Monitoring:
The ability to monitor ecosystems in real time using geospatial data has provided a comprehensive view of environmental changes. This included early detection of changes in vegetation cover, identification

of climate patterns and assessment of the overall health of ecosystems, enabling rapid response to adverse events.

3. Sustainable Use of Water Resources:

The efficient management of water resources has been optimized with geospatial analysis of water bodies. This involved identifying critical aquifer recharge areas, mapping watersheds and assessing water quality. This information supported policies to ensure the sustainable use of water resources in the region.

4. Response to Natural Disasters:

The ability to predict, map and assess risk areas using geospatial data was crucial for responding to natural disasters. This included identifying areas vulnerable to flooding, landslides and forest fires, allowing for the implementation of preventative measures and efficient mobilization in cases of emergencies.

5. Ecological-Economic Zoning:

The implementation of ecological-economic zoning, based on geospatial data, facilitated sustainable territorial planning. This approach considered the distribution of natural resources, environmental limitations and potential economic activities, aiming for a balance between conservation and development.

6. Community Participation:

The transparency provided by management based on geospatial data also promoted community participation. Local communities were empowered with accessible and understandable information about the environment around them, encouraging sustainable practices and the protection of shared natural resources.

Environmental results derived from geospatial data integration demonstrate that this approach not only strengthens environmental management, but also promotes sustainability, resilience and harmony between human communities and natural ecosystems.

15.4. Sustainability and Conservation

Sustainability and Conservation: The Role of Geospatial Data in the Natural Resource Management Project

The application of geospatial data in this specific project is intrinsically aligned with the principles of sustainability and conservation, playing a fundamental role in the long-term preservation of natural resources. Geographic information-based management provides a holistic approach, integrating spatial data to inform strategic decisions and conservation practices. Here are some key aspects of this alliance:

1. Identification of Critical Areas:

Geospatial data analysis allows for the precise identification of critical areas for biodiversity and ecosystems. These areas, often sensitive to human disturbance, are mapped and highlighted, guiding the implementation of protection measures and minimizing negative impacts.

two. Active Monitoring:
Geospatial data enables active and continuous monitoring of environmental changes. This includes detecting deforestation, climate change and other threats to the integrity of natural resources. Real-time monitoring is crucial for rapid responses and effective implementation of conservation strategies.

3. Sustainable Use of Water Resources:
Sustainable management of water resources is promoted through the analysis of geospatial data. Mapping river basins, identifying critical areas and assessing water quality are essential elements. This approach helps to ensure a balance between human demand and the maintenance of aquatic ecosystems.

4. Sustainable Territorial Planning:
The implementation of ecological-economic zoning, based on geospatial data, is a crucial component for sustainable territorial planning. This ensures that economic activities are compatible with environmental conservation, avoiding conflicts and ensuring sustainable land use.

5. Response to Natural Disasters:

The application of geospatial data in risk analysis and response to natural disasters is vital for sustainability. The identification of vulnerable areas, evacuation routes and the efficient allocation of resources in emergency situations contribute to the resilience of local communities and ecosystems.

6. Community Engagement:

The transparency and accessibility provided by geospatial data promotes community engagement. Local communities are trained with information about the importance of natural resources, encouraging sustainable use practices and active protection of the environment.

By aligning natural resource management with sustainability and conservation principles, the application of geospatial data in this project not only optimizes the effectiveness of conservation practices, but also lays a solid foundation for the long-term preservation of the region's valuable natural resources.

15.5. Challenges in Natural Resource Management

Challenges in Natural Resource Management and the Role of Geospatial Data

Natural resource management faces a series of complex challenges, ranging from environmental degradation to conflicts over land use. The application of geospatial data plays a crucial role in overcoming these challenges by providing detailed, location-based insight. Here are some of the common challenges faced in natural resource management and how geospatial data has helped address them:

1. Ambiental degradation:
Challenge: Environmental degradation, including deforestation and soil erosion, threatens the health of ecosystems.
Contribution of Geospatial Data: Analysis of satellite images provides a continuous and detailed view of changes in land use. This helps in identifying critical areas and implementing conservation strategies.

two. Conflicts over Land Use:
Challenge: Conflicts between different stakeholders over land use can result in unsustainable exploitation.
Contribution of Geospatial Data: Clear delimitation of borders, supported by geospatial data, helps to avoid territorial disputes. Location-based ecological-economic zoning contributes to more effective territorial planning.

3. Sustainable Use of Water Resources:

Challenge: The unsustainable use of water resources can lead to scarcity and degradation of water quality.
Contribution of Geospatial Data: River basin analysis and water quality monitoring, using geospatial data, support the sustainable management of water resources. This helps optimize water use and protect aquatic ecosystems.

4. Natural Disaster Risks:
Challenge: Areas prone to natural disasters require an effective response to minimize damage.
Contribution of Geospatial Data: Risk maps based on geospatial data enable the identification of vulnerable areas. This facilitates evacuation planning and resource allocation in emergency situations.

5. Community Engagement:
Challenge: The involvement of local communities is essential for sustainable practices.
Geospatial Data Contribution: Interactive maps and location-based visualizations help effectively communicate the importance of natural resources. Community engagement is strengthened when information is presented in an accessible way.

In addressing these challenges, the intelligent application of geospatial data not only provides a deeper understanding of natural systems, but also empowers managers to make informed and sustainable decisions. The location-based approach contributes to more effective and equitable management of natural resources in the area in question.

Chapter 16: Case Studies 4

16.1. Case 4: Application of Geospatial Data in Logistics and Transport

Case 4: Application of Geospatial Data in Logistics and Transport

Project Context:
Company XYZ, specialized in logistics and transportation, sought to improve its operations through the strategic application of geospatial data. Facing challenges such as route optimization, real-time monitoring and operational efficiency, the company decided to integrate geospatial technologies to address these issues.

Goals:
1. Route Optimization: Use geospatial data to identify the most efficient routes, considering factors such as traffic, road conditions and distances.

2. Real-Time Monitoring: Implement a real-time monitoring system to track the location and status of vehicles in transit.

3. Cost Reduction: Identify opportunities to reduce operational costs, minimizing distances travelled, travel time and fuel consumption.

Geospatial Data Integration:

- Interactive Maps: Implementation of interactive maps that allowed viewing the exact location of vehicles, warehouses and destinations in real time.

- Route Analysis: Use of route optimization algorithms based on geospatial data to calculate the most efficient routes.

- Traffic Alerts: Integration of real-time traffic data to adjust routes and avoid congestion.

Results:
1. Increased Operational Efficiency: Route optimization has led to a significant reduction in travel times and fuel consumption, resulting in more efficient operation.

2. Greater Visibility: Real-time monitoring provided greater visibility into the location and status of each vehicle, allowing quick responses to unexpected events.

3. Cost Reduction: The implementation of optimized routes and monitoring capabilities resulted in an overall reduction in operational costs.

Next steps:
1. Integration with Ordering Systems: Explore the integration of geospatial data with ordering systems to improve demand forecasting and fulfillment efficiency.

2. Sustainability: Investigate ways to use geospatial data to optimize routes with a focus on reducing the carbon footprint.

This case study highlights how the strategic application of geospatial data can transform logistics operations, resulting in improved operational efficiency and positive cost impacts.

16.2. Case Description

Case 4: Application of Geospatial Data in Logistics and Transport

Case Description:
　　　Company ABC, a leader in the retail sector, was facing significant challenges in its supply chain, especially with regard to logistics and transportation. With a vast network of suppliers, warehouses and stores, the company sought to improve operational efficiency and reduce costs in its logistics operations. Faced with these challenges, it was decided to implement a solution based on geospatial data to optimize transportation and improve supply chain management.

Logistics Challenges:

1. Inefficient Routes: The routes used to transport goods were often not the most efficient, resulting in longer delivery times and additional costs.

2. Fleet Management: The company faced difficulties in managing its fleet of vehicles, including a lack of real-time visibility into the location and status of vehicles.

3. Inventory Optimization: Stock management in warehouses and synchronization with store demands needed to be improved to avoid excesses or shortages of products.

Geospatial Data Implementation:
- Route Analysis: Use of route optimization algorithms based on geospatial data to calculate the most efficient routes, considering variables such as traffic, distance and road conditions.

- Real-Time Monitoring: Implementation of a real-time monitoring system that allowed tracking the exact location of vehicles and receiving updates on their status.

- Integration with Stock Systems: Integration of geospatial data with stock systems to improve synchronization between warehouses and store demands.

Results Obtained:

1. Reduction in Transport Costs: Route optimization resulted in a significant reduction in transport costs, minimizing transit time and fuel consumption.

2. Greater Efficiency in Fleet Management: Real-time monitoring provided greater visibility into the location and performance of vehicles, allowing for more efficient fleet management.

3. Inventory Optimization: The integration of geospatial data with inventory systems allowed for better synchronization between supply and demand, avoiding excesses and shortages of products.

This case highlights how the intelligent application of geospatial data in logistics can overcome operational challenges, improve efficiency and result in tangible benefits for a company's supply chain.

16.3. Operational efficiency

Operational Efficiency with the Application of Geospatial Data in Logistics and Transport

Operational efficiency is a vital component to the success of any company, especially in logistics and transport management. In the case of company ABC, the application of geospatial data played a fundamental role in transforming and improving operational efficiency in several aspects.

1. Route Optimization:
- *Cost Reduction:* Geospatial data analysis allowed the optimization of transport routes, taking into account dynamic factors such as traffic, road conditions and precise location of destinations. This resulted in a significant reduction in operational costs associated with transportation.

2. Real-Time Monitoring:
- *Enhanced Visibility:* The implementation of real-time monitoring systems, based on geospatial data, has provided unprecedented visibility into the location and status of vehicles. This improved visibility allowed for more agile and efficient decision-making.

3. Fleet Management:
- *Allocation Efficiency:* Management based on geographic information facilitated the efficient allocation of vehicles to meet the specific demands of routes, customers and cargo volumes. This resulted in more effective use of the available fleet.

4. Inventory Optimization:
- *Synchronization with Demand:* The integration of geospatial data with inventory systems allowed for more precise synchronization between warehouses and store demands. This prevented excess inventory and ensured

products were available when and where they were needed.

5. Location-Based Decision Making:
   - *Informed Decisions:* The ability to visualize data in a geographic context provided a robust basis for decision making. This included choosing the most efficient routes, strategically allocating resources and optimizing logistics processes.

Overall Result:
   The operational efficiency achieved through the intelligent application of geospatial data has had tangible impacts on cost reduction, increased agility in operations and more strategic and efficient supply chain management. The company has experienced significant improvements in its ability to respond to operational challenges, culminating in a more agile and adaptable logistics environment.

16.4. Cost Reduction

Cost Reduction in Logistics and Transport Through Geospatial Data

   The integration of geospatial data in the logistics and transportation sector has had a significant impact on reducing costs, providing operational efficiencies that have translated into tangible economic benefits. Below are some key aspects that contributed to this cost reduction:

1. Route Optimization:
   - *Travel Efficiency:* Geospatial data analysis allowed the identification of the most efficient routes in terms of distance, travel time and traffic conditions. This resulted in direct savings in fuel and vehicle maintenance costs.

2. Delay Prevention:
   - *Anticipation of Adverse Conditions:* Real-time geospatial data enabled the proactive identification of adverse conditions, such as congestion or road works. This ability to anticipate allowed alternative routes and avoided delays, optimizing operational efficiency.

3. Waste Reduction:
   - *Efficient Stock Management:* The use of geospatial data in stock management ensured a more accurate distribution of products. This reduced the need for excessive storage, minimizing waste associated with excess inventory and improving efficiency in moving goods.

4. Strategic Resource Allocation:
   - *Fleet Optimization:* With geospatial data, vehicle allocation can be optimized based on demand, preventing vehicles from traveling long distances without a load. This reduced operating costs and improved fleet usage efficiency.

5. Predictive Maintenance:

- *Reduction in Maintenance Costs:* Predictive analysis based on geospatial data allowed the implementation of preventive maintenance, identifying wear patterns on certain routes. This resulted in reduced costs associated with emergency repairs and extended the useful life of vehicles.

Economic Impact:

The cost reduction derived from the application of geospatial data not only improved profitability, but also contributed to more solid financial management. The operational efficiency achieved provided a competitive advantage, allowing the company to offer more effective and cost-effective services in an increasingly challenging market.

16.5. Innovations in the Transport Sector

Innovations Driven by Geospatial Data in the Transportation Sector

The application of geospatial data has been a key catalyst for numerous innovations in the transportation sector, transforming the way companies operate and deliver services. Below are some of the most significant innovations:

1. Fleet Automation:

- *Real-Time Tracking:* Fleet automation, driven by geospatial data, allows real-time tracking of vehicles. This not only improves fleet visibility, but also makes it possible to monitor the efficiency of each vehicle, prevent delays and optimize routes.

- *Predictive Maintenance Management:* Geospatial data is used for predictive analysis, identifying wear patterns in vehicle components. This makes it possible to carry out preventive maintenance, reducing costs and increasing fleet availability.

2. Intelligent Routing Solutions:
- *Dynamic Route Optimization:* Advanced algorithms based on geospatial data allow dynamic route optimization. This leads to more efficient distribution of goods, saving time and reducing operational costs.

- *Real-Time Considerations:* The ability to integrate real-time data on traffic conditions, weather and unexpected events allows for rapid route adaptations, improving efficiency and reducing the likelihood of delays.

3. Efficient Reverse Logistics:
- *Returns Tracking:* The application of geospatial data in reverse logistics allows you to track returns and waste. This not only simplifies the return process, but also facilitates sustainable waste management.

4. Last Mile Delivery Management:

- *Accurate Routing for Residential Deliveries:* Geospatial data is fundamental in the efficient management of "last mile" delivery. Advanced technologies consider specific characteristics of delivery locations, providing greater precision and efficiency in this critical process.

5. Market Intelligence and Decision Making:
- *Location Data Analysis:* Companies in the transportation sector use geospatial data for market analysis and strategic decision making. This includes identifying new profitable routes, opening new distribution centers and adapting to market demands.

These innovations, driven by geospatial data, are transforming the transportation industry, making it more agile, efficient and sustainable. Continued developments in this area promise not only operational improvements, but also a significant shift in the way we conceive of and experience modern transportation.

Chapter 17: Case Studies 5

17.1. Case 5: Use of Geospatial Data in Urban Planning

Project Description: Use of Geospatial Data in Urban Planning

The project in question focuses on the strategic use of geospatial data to inform and improve urban planning in a growing city. The context involves challenges typical of urban areas, such as the need for sustainable expansion, efficient allocation of resources and ensuring an ideal quality of life for residents.

Goals:
1. Land Use Mapping: Use geospatial data to perform a comprehensive analysis of current land use in the city, identifying residential, commercial, industrial and green areas.

2. Population Density Analysis: Apply geospatial data to analyze population density patterns. This includes identifying densely populated areas as well as locations that could benefit from an increase in urban infrastructure.

3. Infrastructure Planning: Use geographic information to plan and optimize urban infrastructure, including road networks, public transport, water and sewage networks, and leisure areas.

4. Environmental Risk Management: Incorporate geospatial data to map environmental risks, such as floods or landslides, and integrate this information into urban planning to ensure the safety of the population.

5. Sustainable Development: Apply geospatial data to assess the potential for sustainable development, including identifying areas suitable for renewable energy projects, parks and green spaces.

Implementation:
- Data Collection: Geospatial data is collected from multiple sources, including remote sensing, geographic information systems (GIS), and on-site surveys.

- Analysis and Modeling: GIS tools are used to analyze data, create three-dimensional models of the urban environment and perform simulations for different development scenarios.

- Location-Based Decision Making: Urban planning authorities use geographic information to make informed decisions, considering aspects such as accessibility, sustainability and quality of life.

Results:
1. Orderly Development: Urban planning informed by geospatial data has resulted in more orderly and efficient development, avoiding common problems such as congestion and lack of infrastructure.

2. Increased Quality of Life: The efficient allocation of green spaces, improved infrastructure and consideration of environmental factors contributed to a significant increase in the quality of life of residents.

3. Risk Resilience: Risk management based on geospatial data helped the city become more resilient to natural disasters, minimizing impacts and protecting the population.

Next steps:
The project lays a solid foundation for future initiatives, including continually updating geospatial data, implementing emerging technologies, and flexibly adapting to the city's changing needs. The success of this case highlights the critical role of geospatial data in modern urban planning.

17.2. Municipal Experience

Municipal Experience with Geospatial Data in Urban Planning

The municipal experience described in this case highlights the significant transformation achieved by local administration by incorporating geospatial data into its urban planning processes. By integrating geographic information technologies (GIS) and location-based analytics, the administration was able to make more informed and strategic decisions to shape the city's growth and development.

Collection and Use of Data:
The municipal administration began the journey of comprehensive geospatial data collection, gathering information on current land use, population density, existing infrastructure and environmental risks. This data was obtained from multiple sources, including satellite imagery, topographic surveys, and direct surveys.

Analysis and Modeling:
With the implementation of advanced geographic information systems, the administration carried out detailed analysis and three-dimensional modeling of the urban environment. GIS tools allowed the creation of virtual scenarios, making it possible to visualize the potential impact of different development strategies.

Informed Decision Making:
The main change observed was in decision making. Municipal decision-makers began to base their choices on concrete data, considering factors such as accessibility, sustainability and resilience to natural disasters. The strategic use of geographic information allowed a deeper understanding of urban dynamics, guiding long-term development policies.

Tangible Results:

1. Sustainable Development: The city has experienced more sustainable development, with the identification and promotion of suitable areas for green projects and renewable energy.

2. Optimized Infrastructure: The efficient allocation of resources has improved infrastructure, including public transport, road networks and essential services, resulting in a more efficient and connected city.

3. Improved Risk Response: Risk management based on geospatial data has improved the city's response to natural disasters, reducing damage and protecting the population.

Community Engagement:
        The municipal administration also used geospatial data to promote community engagement. Interactive maps and visualizations were shared with citizens, allowing them to understand urban planning decisions and actively participate in the process.

Lessons Learned:
        The experience highlighted the importance of collaboration between sectors, the continuous need for updated data and the flexibility to adapt strategies as the urban environment changes.

The municipal experience reveals how the integration of geospatial data can be a transformative tool in urban planning, creating more resilient, sustainable and future-adapted cities.

17.3. Urban Transformation

Urban Transformation Through the Use of Geospatial Data

In the case presented, the urban transformation driven by the use of geospatial data was a remarkable journey that impacted several areas of urban management, promoting significant changes guided by concrete information. Let's explore how strategically employing this data contributed to transformation in key areas:

1. Infrastructure Development:
The use of geospatial data has catalyzed infrastructure development in a more accurate and efficient way. The municipal administration, armed with detailed information about the urban environment, was able to identify critical areas that required infrastructure improvements, such as water, sewage, electricity and telecommunications networks. The ability to visualize layers of existing and planned infrastructure in a geospatial context has enabled smarter decisions and better coordination between different projects.

two. Strategic Urban Zoning:

Urban zoning, vital for directing growth and ensuring balanced development, has been revolutionized. Using geospatial data, the administration was able to carry out detailed analyzes of each region of the city. This included identifying areas suitable for residential, commercial and industrial use, considering factors such as topography, accessibility and environmental zones. The result was zoning that was more aligned with the needs of the community and the natural characteristics of the land.

3. Smart Urban Mobility:

Geospatial data was fundamental to rethinking urban mobility. With accurate information about traffic, transport patterns and accessibility, the administration was able to optimize routes, improve public transport and plan the development of cycle paths and pedestrian areas. Geospatial visualization enabled a comprehensive analysis of traffic flows, facilitating interventions that significantly improved the fluidity and efficiency of the transport system.

4. Sustainable Development and Green Areas:

Urban transformation included an approach aimed at sustainable development. Geospatial data made it possible to identify suitable areas for parks, green areas and environmental sustainability projects.

The administration was thus able to create a more ecological and resilient city, promoting community well-being and protecting sensitive ecosystems.

5. Community Participation:
Urban transformation did not only occur at the physical level, but also in the involvement and participation of the community. The use of interactive maps and geospatial visualizations allowed citizens to understand planned changes in their areas, contributing valuable feedback and promoting a sense of transparency and participation in the urban transformation process.

Urban transformation driven by geospatial data has not only improved infrastructure and mobility, but also leveraged sustainable development and strengthened the relationship between municipal administration and the community, resulting in a more efficient, equitable and pleasant city to live in.

17.4. Community Involvement

Community Involvement in Urban Planning with Geospatial Data

Community engagement in urban planning, driven by the application of geospatial data, represents a significant shift in the way communities interact and contribute to the development of their areas. Let's explore how transparency and accessibility to geographic data have positively influenced community participation:

1. Access to Transparent Information:

The availability of geospatial data provides communities with transparent access to critical information about urban development. Interactive maps and geospatial visualizations make complex data about building zones, green areas, infrastructure and zoning plans understandable and accessible. This provides community members with a clear and detailed view of what is being proposed, creating a more transparent and understandable environment.

two. Active Participation in Local Decisions:

The application of geospatial data allows citizens to actively participate in decisions related to urban development. With interactive tools, residents can explore project proposals, visualize how these projects will impact their areas, and provide valuable feedback. This direct engagement provides the community with a significant voice in urban planning, contributing to more representative decisions aligned with local needs.

3. Identification of Specific Needs:

Geospatial data analysis allows communities to identify their specific needs more precisely. For example, by viewing areas with deficient green spaces, inadequate infrastructure or mobility issues, residents can highlight their priorities. This collaborative identification of specific needs contributes to more community-centered planning.

4. Reduction of Inequalities and Disparities:
Transparency in geospatial data helps reduce inequalities and disparities in urban development. By viewing information about investments in different areas, community members can ensure development is equitable. This is particularly important to ensure that historically neglected or economically disadvantaged neighborhoods benefit from urban planning fairly.

5. Education and Awareness:
The application of geospatial data not only involves the community in present decisions, but also educates and raises awareness about the urban planning process. By providing detailed information about proposed development, geospatial tools empower citizens to better understand the factors involved, promoting a more informed and engaged community.

Community involvement in urban planning, with the application of geospatial data, strengthens local democracy, builds common understanding and creates more inclusive cities, where decisions reflect the real needs of the community. This collaborative approach represents a positive shift in the way cities are developed and experienced by their inhabitants.

17.5. Planning Challenges

Urban Planning Challenges Using Geospatial Data

The use of geospatial data in urban planning, although it brings significant benefits, is also subject to a number of challenges, especially when applied to complex and growing urban environments. Let's explore some of these challenges:

1. Complexity of the Urban Environment:
Urban environments are inherently complex, with a variety of interconnected factors such as existing infrastructure, construction zones, population density and environmental issues. Geospatial data integration can increase complexity, requiring robust management and analysis systems to ensure information is processed in a meaningful way.

two. Population growth:
Constant and often unplanned population growth presents a significant challenge. Using geospatial data to understand growth patterns, identify areas of densification and plan new infrastructure is crucial. However, the challenge lies in being able to accurately predict future growth, adapting to changing demands and avoiding overloading existing services.

3. Integration of Data from Different Sources:

Geospatial data often comes from multiple sources, such as remote sensors, municipal records, social data, and more. Integrating this data to create a comprehensive view of the urban environment can be challenging due to differences in formats, scales, and accuracies. Effective harmonization is essential to ensure that information is accurate and useful.

4. Sustainable Community Engagement:

While community involvement is a benefit, maintaining that engagement sustainably over time is challenging. Active community participation requires ongoing communication, education and transparency efforts. Additionally, varying opinions within the community can make it challenging to reach consensus on complex urban planning issues.

5. Fast and Dynamic Changes:

Urban environments are subject to rapid changes, such as real estate development, economic changes and unforeseen events. Geospatial data needs to be updated in real time to reflect these changes, and this can be challenging, especially in rapidly developing urban areas.

6. Privacy and Ethics Issues:

The collection and use of geospatial data raises ethical and privacy concerns. Ensuring that data collection and analysis is done ethically and that sensitive information is properly protected is a constant challenge.

7. Resilient Planning:

Developing urban plans that are resilient to extreme events, such as natural disasters, is a growing challenge. Geospatial data plays a key role in preventing and mitigating risks, but the uncertainty inherent in these events adds complexity to the planning process.

Addressing these challenges requires a holistic approach, involving experts in geospatial, urbanism, technology and community engagement to ensure urban planning is sustainable, adaptable and driven by community interests.

Chapter 18: Geospatial Data Tools and Software

18.1. Main Geospatial Database Software

Geospatial database software is an essential tool for storing, managing, and analyzing data that has geographic components. Below are some of the top geospatial database software:

1. PostGIS:
   - Features: PostGIS is a geospatial extension for the PostgreSQL database. It adds geographic data types, spatial indexes, and functions to support geographic data.
   - Capabilities: Provides robust support for complex spatial queries, geographic data analysis, and integration with GIS (Geographic Information Systems) applications.
   - Applications: Widely used in GIS systems, urban planning, natural resource management and related applications.

2. Oracle Spatial:
   - Features: Oracle Spatial is an Oracle Database extension that adds geospatial capabilities to the Oracle database management system.
   - Capabilities: Allows you to store and query geospatial data, supporting advanced spatial operations and integration with GIS applications.
   - Applications: Used in various industries including logistics, telecommunications and asset management.

3. ESRI ArcSDE (Spatial Database Engine):
   - Features: ArcSDE, developed by ESRI, is a technology that allows you to store geographic data in relational databases.
   - Capabilities: Provides a platform to store, retrieve and manage spatial data, integrating with different Database Management Systems (DBMS).
   - Applications: Widely used in GIS solutions, such as ESRI's ArcGIS, for centralized storage of spatial data.

4. GeoServer:
   - Features: GeoServer is an open source server application that allows you to share and edit geospatial data through open standards.
   - Capabilities: Supports publishing geospatial data in standard formats such as Web Map Service (WMS) and Web Feature Service (WFS).
   - Applications: Used to build spatial data infrastructures, provide web mapping services, and collaborate on geospatial projects.

5. MongoDB com GeoJSON:
   - Features: MongoDB is a NoSQL database, and its GeoJSON extension allows efficient storage and querying of geospatial data.
   - Capabilities: Supports spatial indexes, geospatial queries, and analysis operations.
   - Applications: Used in web and mobile applications, Internet of Things (IoT) and in cases where horizontal scalability is a crucial consideration.

6. SQLite with SpatiaLite extension:
   - Features: SQLite is an embedded SQL database, and the SpatiaLite extension adds support for geospatial data.
   - Capabilities: Provides spatial functionalities such as spatial indexes, geospatial operations and support for vector and raster data.
   - Applications: Useful in applications that require a lightweight, embedded solution for geospatial data.

   This software represents a variety of approaches to managing geospatial data, from relational databases with spatial extensions to specialized NoSQL databases. The choice depends on the specific project requirements, the development team's preferences, and the context of use.

18.2. Geographic Visualization Tools

Geographic visualization tools play a crucial role in graphically representing and understanding geospatial data. They are designed to translate complex information into intuitive and interactive visual representations. Below are some of the important aspects of these tools:

1. Interactive Maps:
   - Geographic visualization tools often feature interactive maps that allow users to explore geospatial data dynamically.
   - Users can zoom, pan, click map elements for additional information, and interact directly with the data.

2. Information Layers:
   - These tools support the overlay of multiple layers of geographic information, allowing analysis of data coming from different sources.
   - For example, street layers, administrative boundaries, points of interest and weather data can be combined for a comprehensive analysis.

3. Statistical Data Visualization:
   - In addition to simple geographic representations, tools can incorporate statistical data visualizations such

as bar charts, pie charts, and scatterplots associated with specific locations.

4. Customization of Styles and Symbols:
   - Users can customize the appearance of maps by choosing styles and symbols that best represent the data. This includes defining colors, sizes, and shapes of geographic features.

5. 3D Data Support:
   - Some advanced tools support three-dimensional visualization, allowing users to explore geospatial data in a realistic 3D environment.

6. Spatial Analysis Tools:
   - They include spatial analysis functionalities, such as buffers, proximity analysis and spatial interpolation, which help in understanding geographic patterns and relationships between different elements.

7. Integration with Mapping APIs:
   - Many tools can be integrated with mapping APIs such as Google Maps or Mapbox to enrich the viewing experience and take advantage of location-based services.

8. Mobile Compatibility:
   - Many tools are designed to be responsive, ensuring a consistent viewing experience on mobile devices, which is crucial for mobile apps and solutions.

9. Collaboration and Sharing:
  - Facilitate collaboration and sharing of maps and visualizations, allowing users to easily share their findings and analysis with other interested parties.

10. Support for Various Data Formats:
  - These tools generally support a variety of geospatial data formats, such as GeoJSON, Shapefile, and KML, ensuring compatibility with different data sources.

Geographic visualization tools are essential in many areas, including urban planning, environmental management, logistics, public health and more. They empower users to explore and understand geographic data, providing valuable insights for making informed decisions.

18.3. Spatial Analysis Tools

Spatial analysis tools are essential components in the fields of geoprocessing and geographic information systems (GIS). They enable users to analyze and interpret patterns, relationships and trends in geospatial data, offering a deeper understanding of the geographic environment. Below are some fundamental concepts about these tools:

1. Definition:

- Spatial analysis tools refer to a set of techniques and methods that explore the relationship between geographic data and help in the interpretation of spatial patterns and behaviors.

2. Geoprocessing:
- Spatial analysis is intrinsically linked to geoprocessing, which involves processing geospatial data to obtain valuable information about the distribution, proximity and interaction between elements.

3. Topology and Spatial Relations:
- Spatial analysis tools examine the topology and spatial relationships between different entities, allowing, for example, to identify which elements are close, connected or overlapping.

4. Buffer and Proximity Analysis:
- Buffering is a common technique that creates a zone of influence around a given point, line or polygon. Proximity analysis uses buffers to evaluate which entities are within a certain distance of others.

5. Spatial Interpolation:
- Tools such as spatial interpolation are used to estimate values at unsampled locations based on known values, useful, for example, for predicting the distribution of pollutants or weather patterns.

6. Cluster Analysis (Group):

- Identifies clusters or spatial patterns in data, revealing areas where similar entities are concentrated. This analysis is crucial in fields such as epidemiology to identify disease outbreaks.

7. Route and Accessibility Analysis:
- Spatial analysis tools are also used to optimize routes, assess accessibility and understand how different regions are connected, being useful in logistics, transport and urban planning.

8. Surface Modeling:
- It involves creating three-dimensional surface models from geospatial data, allowing for more realistic visualizations and detailed analysis of terrain features.

9. Geostatistics:
- Uses statistical techniques on geographic data, being valuable for understanding the spatial distribution of phenomena and the variability of these phenomena throughout space.

10. Practical Applications:
- Spatial analysis tools find application in several areas, including environmental management, urban planning, agribusiness, epidemiology, natural resource management, among others.

11. Software SIG:

- Many GIS software, such as ArcGIS, QGIS, and Google Earth Engine, offer a variety of spatial analysis tools, providing users with the ability to comprehensively explore and understand geospatial data.

12. Informed Decision Making:
- Spatial analysis empowers informed decision-making by providing insights that go beyond the simple visual representation of maps, enabling the understanding of hidden patterns and complex relationships between different geographic elements.

Spatial analysis tools are key to transforming geospatial data into meaningful information, providing a deeper, more informed view of the world around us.

18.4. Free Software vs. Commercial

The distinction between free and commercial software in the context of geospatial data is crucial to understanding the options available to professionals working with geographic information. Here are some considerations about each approach:

Software Book:

Benefits:
1. Cost:

- The main benefit of free software is that it is generally free to use. This can be especially appealing to organizations or individual users with limited budgets.

2. Open Source:
   - Free software is generally distributed with its open source code, allowing users to view, modify and distribute the software according to their needs. This promotes transparency and collaboration.

3. Active Community:
   - Many open source projects have active communities of developers and users. This can lead to frequent updates, quick problem resolution, and continuous improvements.

4. Flexibility:
   - The open nature of the code allows users to customize and adapt the software to meet their specific needs.

5. Open Standards:
   - Many open source solutions adhere to open standards, which facilitates interoperability with other tools and data formats.

Disadvantages:
1. Technical Support:
   - Technical support may be limited compared to commercial solutions. Community dependency can result in variable response times.

2. Learning Curve:
   - Some free software may have a steeper learning curve, especially for beginners or non-technical users.

3. Integration with Proprietary Software:
   - There may be challenges in integrating with proprietary software, depending on the data formats and standards used.

Commercial Software:

Benefits:
1. Professional Support:
   - Commercial solutions often offer professional technical support, ensuring quick problem resolution and regular updates.

2. Ease of Use:
   - Many commercial tools are designed to be user-friendly, with intuitive interfaces, making them easy to use for those without advanced technical experience.

3. Integration with Other Tools:
   - Many commercial software are developed to easily integrate with other tools, including design software, CAD (Computer-Aided Design), and databases.

4. Training:

- Many commercial providers offer training programs, making it easier to introduce new users to their platforms.

Disadvantages:
1. Initial Cost:
   - The main drawback is the initial cost. Commercial software often requires a paid license to use, which may be prohibitive for some organizations or individual users.

2. Customization Restrictions:
   - Compared to free software, customization options may be limited as the source code is often not available.

3. Supplier Dependence:
   - Users become dependent on the vendor for updates and ongoing support, which can create vulnerabilities if the vendor stops offering support.

The choice between free and commercial software depends on the specific needs, available resources and user preferences. Many organizations opt for a hybrid approach, using commercial solutions where professional support is crucial and turning to open source solutions to meet specific requirements or for more flexible environments.

18.5. Choosing the Right Tool

Choosing the right tool to deal with geospatial data is crucial to the success of projects related to geoinformation. Here are some important criteria to consider when making this decision:

1. Project Scale:
- Evaluate the scale of your project. Different tools may be better suited for small projects compared to large-scale projects. Make sure the tool you choose can efficiently handle the anticipated volume of data.

2. Required Resources:
- Analyze the specific features you need. This may include spatial analysis capabilities, support for different types of geospatial data (vector, raster, etc.), advanced visualization capabilities, among others. Listing your project's specific requirements will help with selection.

3. Integration with Other Tools:
- Consider how the tool integrates with other tools in your work environment. If you are already using specific software for design, statistical analysis, or databases, make sure your geospatial data tool can efficiently integrate with these solutions.

4. Technical Requirements:
- Check the tool's technical requirements, including operating system compatibility, hardware requirements,

and data standards support. Make sure the tool is technically feasible for your existing infrastructure.

5. Ease of Use:
   - User interface and ease of use are important aspects, especially if the tool will be used by a diverse team who may not have advanced technical experience. Evaluate the learning curve and intuitiveness of the tool.

6. Support and Updates:
   - Consider the availability of technical support. Professionally supported tools can be essential for resolving issues quickly. Additionally, evaluate the regularity of updates, as this indicates the developer's ongoing commitment to improvements and fixes.

7. Costs:
   - Evaluate the costs associated with using the tool, including licenses, maintenance and possible training costs. Consider the return on investment in relation to the resources offered.

8. Data Standards and Formats:
   - Check whether the tool supports open standards and common data formats. This will facilitate interoperability and data exchange with other tools and systems.

9. Ratings and Comments:
   - Search user reviews and comments about the tool. Experiences from other users can provide valuable

insights into the effectiveness and challenges associated with a particular tool.

By considering these criteria, decision makers can make informed decisions about choosing the geospatial data tool best suited for their specific needs.

Chapter 19: Ethics and Privacy in Geospatial Data

19.1. Ethical Issues in Geospatial Data

The use of geospatial data raises several ethical questions that need to be considered to ensure responsible and respectful practices. Some of the key ethical issues associated with geospatial data include:

1. Privacy:
   - Collecting geospatial data can reveal sensitive information about people's locations and movements. The issue of privacy becomes critical, especially when this data is linked to individual identities. It is essential to ensure that data is anonymized or aggregated wherever possible and that strict security measures are in place.

2. Informed Consent:
   - Obtaining informed consent is crucial when collecting geospatial data, especially when it comes to personal information. Users must be fully informed about how their data will be collected, stored and used, and must have the option to grant or refuse consent.

3. Transparency:
   - Organizations that collect and use geospatial data must be transparent about their practices. This includes clearly disclosing the purposes for collecting data, how it will be used and shared, and how individuals can exercise their privacy rights.

4. Fairness and Bias:

- Geospatial data can reflect and even amplify social bias. For example, if certain geographic areas are underrepresented in the data, decisions based on that data may be unfair or discriminatory. Fairness should be a central consideration, and developers should be aware of potential bias in algorithms or data sets.

5. Data Security:
- The security of geospatial data is an essential ethical issue. Data leaks can have serious implications for people's privacy and security in general. Robust cybersecurity measures and secure data management practices are essential.

6. Responsible Use in Military Applications:
- In military contexts, the use of geospatial data raises additional ethical questions, including potential use in operations that may impact the security and well-being of populations. Ethical consideration is crucial when developing and applying geospatial technologies in military contexts.

7. Access and Inequality:
- The availability of geospatial data and access to associated technologies can vary significantly between different regions and social groups. This can contribute to disparities and inequalities. Ensuring that access to and benefits associated with geospatial data are distributed fairly is an important ethical consideration.

8. Responsibility in Automated Decisions:

- Automation based on geospatial data, such as in self-driving cars, raises ethical questions about who is responsible in the event of accidents or failures. Clear assignment of responsibility and ethical consideration in automated decision making are critical.

By addressing these ethical issues, developers, researchers, and organizations can contribute to the responsible and ethical use of geospatial data, promoting public trust and minimizing potential negative impacts.

19.2. Privacy and Location Data

The relationship between privacy and location data is a growing concern as the collection and use of geospatial information becomes more widespread. Here are some key points about this relationship:

1. Tracking and Identification:
- Collecting location data can enable precise tracking of individual movements. This raises concerns about privacy, as location can be highly sensitive information. When combined with other data, personal identification can become possible, revealing details about a person's daily life.

2. Balance between Utility and Privacy:

- Many services and applications based on location data offer significant benefits, such as efficient navigation, personalized recommendations and location services. However, this benefit often requires sharing location data. Finding the right balance between the usefulness of these services and the protection of privacy is a challenge.

3. Informed Consent:

- Informed consent is key when it comes to location data. People must be fully informed about how their location data will be collected, used and shared. They must have the option to grant or deny that consent, and revoking consent must be a clear option.

4. Anonymization and Data Aggregation:

- To protect privacy, organizations can adopt practices such as anonymization and data aggregation. Anonymization removes or alters identifiable information, while aggregation groups data to make it impossible to identify information specific to an individual.

5. Data Security:

- The security of location data is vital to prevent unauthorized access and leaks. Organizations must implement robust cybersecurity measures to protect this sensitive information.

6. Data Retention Policies:

- Establishing clear data retention policies is essential. Keeping location data longer than necessary can increase privacy risks. Setting specific periods for retention and securely deleting data after that period is good practice.

7. User Education:
- User education plays a crucial role. Users need to understand how their location data is used, how they can control their privacy settings, and what the risks and benefits associated with sharing location data are.

8. Ethical and Legal Standards:
- Compliance with ethical and legal standards is essential. Regulations such as the General Data Protection Regulation (GDPR) in the European Union establish strict guidelines for the collection and processing of personal data, including location data.

The relationship between privacy and location data highlights the importance of ethical and transparent approaches to collecting and using this information, ensuring that the usefulness of location-based services does not compromise individual privacy.

19.3. Regulations and Compliance

Regulation and compliance regarding geospatial data are intrinsically linked to the protection of privacy and ethics in the collection, processing and use of this information. Several jurisdictions have established laws and guidelines to ensure the protection of individual rights and data security. Here are some relevant points:

1. General Data Protection Regulation (GDPR - European Union):
    - The GDPR is one of the most comprehensive legislations regarding the protection of personal data. It applies to location data and establishes principles such as informed consent, the right to access, rectify and delete data, and the obligation to notify data breaches.

2. Privacy Laws in the United States:
    - In the United States, there is no specific comprehensive federal data privacy law, but some state laws, such as the California Consumer Privacy Act (CCPA), impose specific requirements regarding privacy and consumer control over their data.

3. General Personal Data Protection Law (LGPD - Brazil):
    - The LGPD, inspired by the GDPR, is Brazilian legislation that deals with the protection of personal data, including location data. It establishes data subject rights, principles of transparency and finality, and requires security measures to protect that data.

4. Privacy Protection Laws in Asia Pacific:
    - Several countries in the Asia-Pacific region, such as Japan, South Korea, and Australia, have privacy laws

that cover the collection and use of personal data, including location data.

5. ISO 37120 - Sustainable Cities Indicators:
   - ISO 37120 is an international standard that defines indicators for sustainable cities, including those related to geospatial data. This standard provides a set of standards to ensure the quality and reliability of urban data.

6. Artificial Intelligence Ethical Guidelines:
   - As technologies such as machine learning and artificial intelligence are applied to geospatial data, ethical guidelines specific to these technologies also become relevant. Organizations and researchers are developing guidelines to ensure the ethical use of these technologies.

7. Data Minimization Principles:
   - Many regulations emphasize the principle of data minimization, encouraging the collection of only the data necessary for the specific purpose. This applies equally to geospatial data, where excessive information collection is seen as an unethical practice.

8. Privacy Impact Assessment (PIA):
   - Some jurisdictions and standards recommend conducting Privacy Impact Assessments to assess risks and mitigate potential adverse privacy impacts before undertaking certain data processing activities, including geospatial data.

The regulatory landscape reflects global recognition of the importance of protecting privacy in geospatial data, with different regions adopting specific approaches to promote compliance and ethics in the use of this information.

19.4. Corporate social responsibility

Corporate social responsibility (CSR) in the context of geospatial data involves ethical consideration of the social impact of activities related to the collection, processing and use of this data. Here are some ways organizations can adopt ethical practices in geospatial data:

1. Transparency and Communication:
   - Organizations must be transparent about how they collect, process and use geospatial data. Clear communication with stakeholders, including the general public, is essential to building trust.

2. Informed Consent:
   - Organizations must seek informed consent from users for the collection and use of geospatial data whenever applicable. This ensures that individuals are aware of and agree to the use of their location information.

3. Data Minimization:

   - Ethical practices involve data minimization, that is, collecting only the geospatial data necessary for the specific purpose. This reduces the risk of misuse or excessive collection of information.

4. Data Security:

   - The security of geospatial data is crucial. Organizations must implement robust security measures to protect this information from unauthorized access, ensuring data privacy and integrity.

5. Equity and Inclusion:

   - Organizations must ensure that the collection and use of geospatial data is equitable and inclusive. This means considering how practices affect different social groups and ensuring there is no discrimination.

6. Privacy Impact Assessment (PIA):

   - Conducting Privacy Impact Assessments helps identify and mitigate privacy risks associated with the collection and use of geospatial data. This practice is especially important in large-scale projects.

7. Community Collaboration:

   - Collaboration with the local community is an ethical practice. Organizations can involve the community in the decision-making process about how geospatial data will be used in their environment, considering their opinions and needs.

8. Education and Awareness:
   - Organizations have a responsibility to educate their employees, customers and the wider community about the ethical implications of geospatial data. This includes promoting awareness about privacy, security and social impact.

9. Compliance with Regulations and Laws:
   - Complying with local and international standards and laws related to privacy and data protection is a fundamental part of corporate social responsibility. This involves staying up to date with changing regulations and adjusting practices as necessary.

Corporate social responsibility in the context of geospatial data not only addresses ethical considerations, but also builds a solid foundation of trust between organizations and their stakeholders, contributing to a more ethical and sustainable data environment.

19.5. Ethical Recommendations

Handling geospatial data ethically is critical to protecting privacy, ensuring fairness, and building public trust. Here are some ethical recommendations to guide the collection, use, and sharing of geospatial data:

1. Transparency and Communication:
   - Be transparent about how geospatial data is collected, processed and used. Provide clear information to users, explaining the purposes of collection and how the data will be used.

2. Informed Consent:
   - Seek informed consent whenever possible. Allow users to have control over their location information and provide clear options to opt-in or opt-out of geospatial data collection.

3. Data Minimization:
   - Collect only the geospatial data necessary for the specific purpose. Avoid excessive or indiscriminate collection of information, thus minimizing the risks of misuse.

4. Data Security:
   - Implement robust security measures to protect geospatial data from unauthorized access. Ensure data is stored and transmitted securely, reducing the risk of security breaches.

5. Equity and Inclusion:
   - Consider the differential impacts that geospatial data practices may have on different social groups. Avoid practices that could result in discrimination or

inequalities and promote equity in access and use of data.

6. Privacy Impact Assessment (PIA):
   - Conduct Privacy Impact Assessments to identify and mitigate privacy risks associated with the collection and use of geospatial data. This is particularly important in large-scale projects.

7. Anonymization and Pseudonymization:
   - To the maximum extent possible, anonymize or pseudonymize geospatial data to protect the identity of individuals. This reduces the possibility of directly tracking information to specific people.

8. Community Collaboration:
   - Involve the community in the decision-making process about the collection and use of geospatial data in their environment. Consider community concerns and needs to ensure an inclusive approach.

9. Education and Awareness:
   - Educate employees, users and stakeholders about the importance of privacy and ethics in geospatial data. Promote awareness of the social and individual impacts of these practices.

10. Corporate Social Responsibility:
   - Adopt corporate social responsibility practices when dealing with geospatial data. Consider not only legal

obligations but also the broader social impact of your activities.

11. Regulatory Compliance:
- Strictly comply with local and international regulations related to privacy and geospatial data protection. Stay up to date on changing laws and adjust practices as needed.

By following these ethical recommendations, organizations can contribute to building a more ethical, transparent and trustworthy geospatial data environment, promoting the responsible and equitable use of this information.

Chapter 20: Conclusion and Future Prospects

20.1. Impact of Geospatial Data

Geospatial data has played a fundamental role in transforming how we understand, interact and address a variety of challenges across different sectors of society. Geoinformation, which includes geospatial data such as maps, geographic coordinates and location information, has significant impacts on decision-making, planning and innovation in several areas. Let's explore the impact of this data on some key sectors:

1. Urban Planning:
    - Geoinformation is essential in urban development and planning. It provides detailed insights into land use, population density and existing infrastructure.
    - Enables the identification of risk areas, facilitating sustainable development and disaster mitigation.

2. Logistics and Transport:
    - Geospatial data optimizes logistics operations, providing detailed information on routes, traffic and road conditions.
    - Contribute to transport efficiency, cost reduction and improvements in the delivery of goods.

3. Precision Agriculture:

- Information about soil, climate and topography, collected through geospatial data, is crucial in precision agriculture.
- Optimize the use of resources, improve the efficiency of agricultural practices and reduce environmental impact.

4. Natural Resource Management:
- Geospatial data is fundamental in the sustainable management of ecosystems, biodiversity and water resources.
- Facilitate informed decision-making for environmental preservation and monitoring.

5. Public Health:
- They allow mapping disease patterns and air quality, helping to formulate public health strategies.
- They are crucial in emergency situations, helping to locate medical resources and distribute aid efficiently.

6. Energy Sector:
- In the energy industry, geospatial data is used for the optimal location of facilities such as wind farms and solar plants.
- Contribute to the management of electrical networks and the prevention of natural disasters.

7. Education and Research:
- They facilitate the visualization and understanding of complex geographic phenomena, supporting teaching and research activities.

- They are valuable for environmental, climatic and geological studies.

8. Public Safety:
- Geospatial data assists in public security operations, allowing the visualization of crime areas, planning routes for emergency responses and management of large-scale events.

9. Business and Marketing:
- They are used to analyze customer location, identify market opportunities and develop business expansion strategies.
- Location-based mobile apps and online services directly benefit from this data.

10. Science and Space Research:
- They play a crucial role in space missions, from precisely locating probes to analyzing data collected from other celestial bodies.

Geospatial data has a profound influence on virtually every sector of modern society. Its ability to provide detailed information about the world around us drives innovation, improves efficiency and empowers more informed decision-making on local and global scales. The continued advancement of these technologies promises even more positive contributions to the way we understand and interact with our planet.

20.2. The Future of Geoinformation

The future of geoinformation is exciting, driven by a convergence of emerging technologies, significant advancements, and trends that will shape how we use and understand geospatial data. Several perspectives can be explored:

1. Artificial Intelligence and Machine Learning (AI/ML):
   - AI and ML will play a central role in geospatial data analysis, enabling deeper insights and process automation.
   - Advanced algorithms will be able to identify complex patterns and predict changes across geographic and temporal scales.

2. Augmented and Virtual Reality (AR/VR):
   - The integration of AR and VR with geospatial data will provide immersive experiences for users, allowing the three-dimensional visualization of geographic information.
   - These technologies will be fundamental in urban planning, tourism and training environments.

3. Predictive Analysis and Big Data:

- Predictive analytics will continue to evolve, offering the ability to anticipate geographic events, from climate change to traffic patterns.
- Big Data environments will allow real-time processing of large volumes of geospatial data.

4. Redes 5G:

- The widespread implementation of 5G networks will enable faster transmission and reception of real-time geospatial data.
- Sectors such as transport, healthcare and emergency will benefit from ultra-fast connectivity for instant decision making.

5. Sensors and IoT:

- The increase in the number of sensors and IoT devices will collect geospatial data in real time, providing a more dynamic view of the environment.
- Agricultural, environmental and public safety sectors will benefit from continuous monitoring.

6. Blockchain for Geospatial Dice:

- Blockchain technology can be employed to guarantee the integrity and authenticity of geospatial data, providing a transparent and unalterable record.
- This is crucial in applications such as land ownership and government records.

7. Smart Cities and Mobility:

- The development of smart cities will rely heavily on geospatial data to optimize infrastructure, urban services and mobility.
- The integration of autonomous vehicles and intelligent transportation systems will rely heavily on this data.

8. Collaboration and Open Standards:
- Collaboration between organizations and the adoption of open standards will be crucial to ensuring interoperability and efficient exchange of geospatial data.
- Global initiatives may emerge to standardize the collection, storage and sharing of geographic information.

9. Privacy and Ethics:
- Privacy concerns will increase as more location data is collected. New regulations and ethical practices will emerge to protect individuals.
- Anonymization and data control tools may become more prominent.

10. Education and Awareness:
- Geoinformation education will become a fundamental part of curricula in various fields, enabling professionals to understand and use geospatial data effectively.

These perspectives represent only an initial glimpse of what is to come. The future of geoinformation will certainly be characterized by continuous innovations, global collaboration and an increasingly deeper understanding of our world through geospatial data.

20.3. Encouragement for Continued Exploration

Dear reader,

By embarking on the fascinating journey of geospatial data, you are opening the doors to a vast universe of discoveries, innovations, and impactful applications. Continued exploration in this dynamic field offers opportunities for professional growth and contributes to significant advancements across diverse industries.

1. Multidisciplinary Research:
   - Explore the intersections between geospatial data and other disciplines such as computer science, biology, economics, and sociology. Many advances occur in areas of convergence.

two. Technological Innovations:
   - Be aware of the latest technological innovations such as artificial intelligence, machine learning and augmented reality. These technologies are shaping the future of geospatial data.

3. Emerging Applications:

- Continuous research into emerging applications such as smart cities, precision agriculture and location-based healthcare offers opportunities to develop innovative solutions.

4. Participation in Communities:

- Engage in geoinformation communities, participate in conferences, workshops and online forums. Exchanging ideas with peers and experts drives learning and discovery.

5. Continuing Education:

- Stay up to date with evolving courses and certifications in the field of geospatial data. Continuing education is crucial to keep up with rapid changes in technologies and practices.

6. Open Data Exploration:

- Leverage the benefits of available open geospatial data. Many organizations and governments share valuable data sets that can be explored for personal studies and projects.

7. Practical Projects:

- Put your knowledge into practice through personal projects. Developing practical solutions to geospatial challenges reinforces learning and can result in significant contributions.

8. Ethical Awareness:

- Be aware of ethical considerations in collecting and using geospatial data. Ethical and responsible development is vital to ensuring trust and widespread acceptance of these technologies.

9. Taking Advantage of Professional Opportunities:

- Be aware of professional opportunities in companies, government organizations and research sectors that are looking for experts in geospatial data. Your knowledge can be a valuable asset.

10. Knowledge Sharing:

- Contribute to the community by sharing your knowledge. Blogs, articles, and tutorials can not only solidify your understanding but also benefit other professionals and enthusiasts.

In this vast field of geospatial data, exploration is a constant journey of learning and discovery. By staying curious, fresh, and committed, you will not only expand your skills but also play a significant role in advancing this dynamic discipline.

Keep exploring, innovating and contributing to the exciting world of geospatial data.

With enthusiasm,
Geo Report Collaborators

www.ingramcontent.com/pod-product-compliance
Lightning Source LLC
La Vergne TN
LVHW051222050326
832903LV00028B/2212